Penguin Special S235
Why Liberal ?
Harry Cowie

Harry Cowie is Director of Research at Liberal Party
Headquarters, where for the last four years he has been
responsible for drafting policy reports and supplying briefing
material for the Liberal Parliamentary Party. He also takes
part in the N.A.T.O. Parliamentarians' Conference, where he
acts as secretary to the Economic Committee.

Educated at Glasgow University and Balliol College,
Oxford, he spent a year in North America after National
Service, training as investment analyst. He then spent three
years in the City, where he became interested in the Common
Market which was being set up, and left the City to take
part in a study of Britain and the Common Market at
Political and Economic Planning (P.E.P.), where he was a
senior research adviser for three years.

Harry Cowie is thirty-four years old, was born in
Scotland, and is married to a New Zealander, who compères
a weekly television programme. They have a young baby.

Harry Cowie

Why Liberal?

Penguin Books

Penguin Books Ltd, Harmondsworth, Middlesex, England
Penguin Books Inc., 3300 Clipper Mill Road, Baltimore 11, Md, U.S.A.
Penguin Books Pty Ltd, Ringwood, Victoria, Australia

First published 1964

Copyright © Harry Cowie, 1964

Made and printed in Great Britain
by Cox and Wyman Ltd,
London, Reading, and Fakenham
Set in Intertype Plantin

Contents

Preface

This book attempts to set down the most compelling reasons for voting Liberal at the next General Election. It is not an authoritative guide to Liberal policy – this has already been published in a series of reports and pamphlets and summarized in the draft programme *Partners in a New Britain*. Nor does this book attempt to cover every aspect of Liberal policy. Most of the topics, such as the Health Service, which are omitted have in any case been the subject of comprehensive Liberal proposals. The book is necessarily, therefore, a personal statement and in no way commits the Liberal party, although I have tried to indicate when I am putting forward Liberal policy as such. While it does not commit the Party I would like to express my thanks to the members of various policy committees and my colleagues in the Liberal Research Department on whose views I have drawn heavily. I would like to express my debt to my wife as this book has been written at home, owing to pressure of work, in a few weeks; which I hope will explain the inadequacies.

1: Introduction

A hundred years ago Britain led the world in prosperity and power. Today it has become an also-ran. Materially the country which led the first industrial revolution lags behind in the second. Socially the class barriers inherited from another age divide our society and prevent our people from enjoying to the full the opportunities that could be open to all. Politically our traditional machinery of government has become ossified and discredited. In the world at large our country has lost the power it once possessed in the age of the nation state, without taking on the new role it could assume in the creation of a partnership between nations.

Britain can no longer be top nation, but we can still be a first-rate country. We live in an age when modern technology could transform our lives, where there is no economic or technical necessity for wealth or education to remain the privilege of part of the community. The social barriers that thwart so many lives in Britain and cause us to live in a split society of 'us' and 'them' are man-made and can still be changed. We can still play a leading role in creating an international community. Our future depends on our ability to replace the class divisions, the squalor, and the apathy of life today with a new sense of partnership, participation, and social justice.

But there will be no fundamental change so long as we continue to withdraw into insularity and cling to delusions of grandeur. Britain can be again a first-rate country, but our role will depend on the quality of our education, industry, and science; on the democratic quality and efficiency of our government; on the fairness of our judicial system; on the vitality of our arts and architecture; and above all on mutual tolerance and our determination to trust one another in establishing a firm partnership both inside the country and with other like-minded nations abroad.

So long as we pursue our past we shall decline. Britain can no longer rule the world and impose its way of life and institutions upon other nations nor can our country afford to make the wrong use of its economic resources in a nuclear arms race. Britain is in great danger of retreating into the past, withdrawing from the modern world, and seeking a substitute for our imperial yesterday in Commonwealth dreams of tomorrow. We shall succeed in harnessing modern technology only if we create a society which is open to new ideas and has a vigour and honesty of intellectual life. This means keeping our international outlook and using it as a spur for making improvements in our way of life. For it is not so much lack of resources that has caused Britain to stagnate but Conservative attitudes, resistance to change, and lack of skill in making the best use of modern methods and equipment.

Which political party in Britain has the will to break with the attitudes and muddled thinking that has done duty for policy in the past? The Conservatives promise us that they will modernize Britain but fail to say why they have done so little to keep us up to date in the last thirteen years. The reasons are very obvious. The Conservative party represents the established monied interests in Britain and it is precisely because these interests are clinging to the past that Britain has been lagging behind. The Establishment does not lack talent, but it has failed to understand the new technological revolution because it has turned its back on a professional approach. The Tory party is dominated by old Etonians, the Civil Service by arts-trained administrators, and British industry by men who, if they are not public-school boys themselves, have imbibed an anti-professional attitude to science and technology. This ruling clique does, however, believe in one kind of expertise – financial techniques – which stems from the fact that Britain became rich and great during the mercantile period. Although the first industrial revolution created a new group of business men, London – and especially the City – has tended to dominate British economic and political life. The northern and midland manufacturers had to come to the City for finance and they sent their children to public schools and ancient universities for social recognition, where they learnt that it was socially acceptable to be merchant bankers, senior civil servants, or classical dons, but not technicians. The 'City' mentality of the Conservative party has misled it into holding back expansion in order to keep up the myth of the £. It has pursued economic policies which have created the largest capital gains in British history but which have also kept Britain at the bottom of the international league tables in almost every indicator of economic performance. The result is that squalor has spread, the social services have been lagging behind, and more working days have been lost in industrial action than since the General Strike in 1926. The Conservative party has demonstrated for too long that it does not want to adapt to a changing world.

The Labour party is also dominated by established interests which, in the words of Mr Anthony Crosland, M.P., 'manifest a colossal resistance to change'. The Labour movement is still dominated by the power of the mass of trade unions which are scared of the technological revolution that they realize could upset their, until recently, unchallenged place in the political economy of this country.

As everyone knows, the British Labour party has never been a revolutionary party, but its inability to rethink its policies and offer the country a radical alternative to Conservatism has resulted in defeats in three successive general elections. Its leaders today – and especially Mr Harold Wilson – indulge in a dangerous kind of double talk by which they try to keep the divergent wings of their party together. In an effort to keep up a semblance of party unity they have adopted a little-Englander outlook in international affairs which perhaps provides a substitute for the grandeur of the past (which the British working class has always enjoyed) but freezes the nation into an insular posture which, to quote Sir Geoffrey Crowther, will result in the long run in Britain being to 'the world of the twenty-first century what Spain was to the eighteenth'.

More and more people are realizing that only a party which has a strong sense of liberal values and no vested interests to protect will create a new spirit of partnership out of our class-ridden society and let us all take advantage of what modern life has to offer. It must also be a party which understands and is in sympathy with the key social group in the new technological revolution, namely the rising group of technicians, teachers, managers, and scientists. Their recruitment, their education, their culture, their élan, will become more crucial for our society as a whole as the world enters upon an era of the fuller application of modern scientific discoveries and techniques to every aspect of our lives, Finally and equally important, it must be a party which can give Britain the kind of role which a lively country can play in creating a more closely integrated world. The Liberal party has been attracting support because it does want to create a new spirit of partnership and puts the consumer before vested interests. An editorial in the *Spectator* (of all papers) emphasized this point last September.

The Liberals' strongest card is precisely that they have no vested interests to protect and can therefore claim to be the only party which is free to come to current problems with an open mind. It is a card which neither Labour not Tories can easily wrest from them. . . .

The political correspondent of the *Financial Times,* another paper which cannot be accused of Liberal bias, wrote at the time of the 1963 Liberal Assembly:

Liberals have been asking in public some of the fundamental questions which now trouble people of all political persuasions – and they have been asking them with a degree of intellectual freedom which would be impossible for either the Tories or the Socialists. . . . They [the Liberals] have a widespread appeal to politically self-conscious and uncommitted people in the country. The Liberals are a new and 'classless' party, and that is both a strength and a weakness. . . . It is the new 'classless' who are the floating voters – the men and women to whom Tories and Socialists as well as the Liberal Party must appeal. And these people, unwedded to tradition (whether of trade-union or public-school society) and impatient with the old and apparently creaking political institutions, are far more prepared to question the bases on which our society rests. The Liberals are well prepared to voice these questions for them. (13 September 1963.)

It is the new 'classless' people of Britain who are going to decide the future of this country. The fact that it is the Liberal party which is attracting the vote of these New Men has not gone unnoticed by the other two parties. Mr Woodrow Wyatt was reported in the *Observer* of 18 March 1962 as saying: 'There is a new social group emerging. It is young. It is white-collar. It is skilled. It is ambitious to advance socially and economically. It will decide the next election. It does not want the Tories but it does not want a cloth-cap Labour party either.' At the 1962

Conservative Party Conference Mr Angus Maude, M.P., said: 'Whereas 15 years ago thousands of young people were joining the Tories, today they are turning Liberal.' In an analysis of a nation-wide survey of the Floating Voter published in the *Sunday Times* on 17 March 1963, Mr David Butler showed that Liberals were rated by the supporters of all three parties as more up-to-date than any of the others. The survey also showed that Liberals come nearest to attracting equal support from all members of the community.

2: Modernizing Government

The building of a new Britain depends not only on ideas but on getting things done. At the heart of the problem of the post-war years has been a vacuum in our economic and industrial policy. Yet what stands in the way of getting things done is the machinery of government itself. 'Parliamentary government has already very largely perished,' wrote a former Conservative M.P., Christopher Hollis, in a Liberal pamphlet. 'The Member is the obedient servant of the party machine. He tramps into the division lobby for or against he knows not what upon subjects which as a general rule no opinion save that of the specialist is of the least value.' *

Power has shifted to the Prime Minister and the Civil Service. Legislation is passed with only minor amendments, and there is almost no scope for private Members' Bills, unless the Government finds them convenient. The Executive is no longer even required to explain its policies and intentions in major questions. If it had not been for the Liberal M.P.s the question of Britain entering into negotiations with the European Economic Community would not have been debated until the Prime Minister announced on 31 July 1961 that 'after long and careful consideration Her Majesty's Government have come to the conclusion that it would be right for Britain to make applications under Article 237'. As it was, the two-day debate after the 'long and careful consideration' was the first full debate on what many believe to be the most important issue which has come before Parliament since the war. No effective way has been found of controlling the nationalized industries or curbing wasted Government expenditure. More than £1,000 million was squandered in the 1955 Modernization Plan for British Railways. The Government hailed it at the time as a 'courageous and imaginative plan': it transpired five years later that it had been prepared on medieval accounting methods. Before 1959 British Railways had a curious way of calculating a reduction in a pros-

* Christopher Hollis, *Can Parliament Survive*, p.64 (Liberal Publication Dept).

pective loss or profit. No wonder the arrival of Dr Beeching, who has only applied the standard techniques of operational analysis to British Railways, has created such a furore. The amazing point which emerges from the Select Committee Report on the Railways is that not only the House of Commons but the Ministry of Transport did not know the basis on which the Modernization Plan had been drawn up: 'it became doubtful whether the Plan would bring in the profits that had been hoped for ... and the Ministry began to ask for a much more detailed justification of the schemes on which the money was to be spent'.

Not only is the executive not under vigorous democratic control but it is inefficient and uncoordinated, and it frequently makes the wrong decisions or fails to communicate the right decisions to the public. This is not because top civil servants are inefficient or unintelligent. The reverse is true. But the machinery of the Civil Service and its tradition are Victorian in outlook. The Victorian idea was that administrators should be chosen not with special experience of any kind but as intelligent, well-educated amateurs. The result is that of the 280 recruits to the Civil Service Administrative Class between 1957 and 1962 only nine had a scientific background. Apart from the Treasury and the Ministry of Agriculture there are only four full-time economists in Government service, and there are none in the Board of Trade, the Ministries of Transport and Housing, or the Inland Revenue. Is it really any wonder that Britain has failed to formulate any effective anti-monopolies legislation, a coordinated transport system, an efficient building industry, or a simplified tax system?

The Commons

What is even stranger is the belief on the part of the Conservative and Labour parties that they can modernize Britain without first modernizing the machinery of government. It was Mr Harford Thomas who pointed out in a recent *Guardian* pamphlet, *A New Britain*, that:

the first section of the Liberal Programme, *Partners in a New Britain*, deals with the reform of Parliament, the Civil Service, and local government. The opening session of this year's [1963] Liberal Assembly was devoted to parliamentary, administrative and electoral reform and a large part of the second session, on planning, was concerned with the structure of government.

This order of priorities must have puzzled Conservative Central Office and Transport House, for the reorganization of the machinery of government is not even a minor theme in their published programmes or in their conference debates. Evidently neither of the two big parties thinks it worth perplexing the voter with the arguments over the technicalities of government.

Could it be that the two other parties are advocating modernization only as a good selling line; and that they have not really thought through all the implications? Or is it possible that the Tory and Labour parties, as full members of the Club, feel that changes are not desirable? Certainly the Tories have made very little attempt, apart from the Peerage Act, to improve the parliamentary set-up. Their M.P.s seem quite happy with the system, especially as in the first six and a half years of the present administration Tory M.P.s, past and present, received 27 peerages, 30 baronetcies, and 48 knighthoods, which means that one in three was elevated.

Twelve years in opposition have not wrung any ideas out of the Labour party on the machinery of government. According to Mr Crossman, 'Under the Attlee Government . . . it was difficult to raise the faintest interest . . . [yet] more time is wasted and more energy and more talent frustrated in the British Parliament than in any other organization of which I have had any experience.' The situation is not very different today. Both Mr Wilson and Mr Bowden, the Labour Chief Whip, are on record as not being in favour of changes in the parliamentary system.

Liberals, by contrast, believe that the whole machinery of Parliament needs to be radically overhauled. Greater use should be made of the Standing Committee system, partly to allow more time for general debates and partly to ensure that legislation of a specialized or technical nature is thoroughly examined by M.P.s whose knowledge and experience qualify them for the job. These Committees would be able to draw upon the advice of experts and cross-examine senior civil servants in the major fields of policy – economics, defence, foreign policy. Greater use of the Committee system would allow backbencher M.P.s opportunities to influence legislation behind the scenes and would allow more time for the introduction of private Members' Bills on the floor of the House. More free votes would also restore reality to debates. A government should not be compelled to resign by a hostile vote except on a vote of confidence.

The pay and conditions of M.P.s must be improved in order to increase the efficiency and drawing power of the House of Commons. It is interesting to note that the two issues when backbench M.P.s have played a vital role in recent years – commercial TV. and Katanga – were both results of backing by pressure groups outside Parliament. Indeed, according to Professor Beer, if we had some way of measuring political power we could possibly demonstrate that at the present time pressure groups are more powerful in Britain than in the United States. Liberals do not regard this as a healthy development. Too often the consumer is not organized, and whereas producer groups bombard M.P.s with facts and figures the average citizen does not get his point of view recorded. M.P.s should not have to supplement their pay by offering their services as Public Relations Officers, nor should they have to depend on organized groups for their information.

The Lords

The House of Lords, with the exceptions of the life peers and its reduced delaying powers, has remained unchanged since the Liberal party forced through the Parliament Act of 1911. There is no place in a new Britain for a second chamber where the majority of members hold a seat by virtue of birth. Either members of the second chamber should be appointed on grounds of personal distinction or public service, and selected in such a way that a permanent majority is not assured to any political party, or they should be elected on a regional basis. If a majority of members were drawn from the different regions of Britain, it would be possible to have a clearer reflection of regional interests in Parliament. The absence of regional representation has allowed the post-war governments to take an over-centralized view of the country's real interests. It was not till the publication of the N.E.D.C. Report on *Conditions Favourable to Faster Growth* that it became obvious, for instance, that the creation of 200,000 new jobs in the next four years need only cost £20 million net, whereas in 1962 £38 million was spent in unemployment benefits and national assistance to unemployed persons in development districts. The Liberal party had called in 1962 for regional development plans and the development of new towns and major 'magnet' areas throughout the country in order to attract industry and population and check the present drift to over-populated areas, particularly the south-east. Liberal M.P.s put down an amendment to the 1963 Finance Bill calling for greater inducements for growth points. This was rejected by the Government at the time but was later incorporated in the regional development plans for Scotland and the north-east in November 1963. The continuing high level of unemployment in these areas makes quick Government action necessary before the General Election, in spite of promises in the 1959 Conservative Manifesto that regional employment would be a top priority. A strong regional representation in the second chamber could have made it more difficult for the Government to ignore positive regional action for so long.

Reform of the second chamber to take account of regional interests would not shift more power to the regions themselves unless the second chamber was given the powers of the U.S. Senate. To do this, however, would be to reverse the balance of power between the Commons and the second chamber, which would be a complete mistake in a country the size of Britain. It is only historically valid in America because the Senate was created to preserve the identity of sovereign states within a federation and only survives because of the diversity of interests within a country which stretches across a continent.

The Regions

Power needs to be brought directly to the regions of Britain. Regional planning authorities should be set up which are directly responsible to the regions they represent. People will not be encouraged to participate in the activity of regional regeneration unless the various processes of government are brought as close to the people as possible. Good government, at the regional as well as the national level, must begin with a vision of the country we want to build. Unless the men of the West Country are made to feel that their homes, jobs, and schools are their responsibility, regional plans will not spark off regional development.

So long as power is centralized in London, people will inevitably drift to the south-east. It is not sufficient to set up regional offices of the Whitehall Ministries, for the big boys who want quick decisions will still be constantly on the train to London to obtain a personal decision from a key official at the Ministry. The regional planning authorities must have clear responsibility for the functions which need to be planned and controlled within the regional boundaries. They should draw up plans for their regions' transport, location of industry, town and country planning, and education.

Some of these powers are at present decided in Whitehall. At present Whitehall Ministries are responsible for allocating school building funds and industrial location certificates and hospital building funds, but many of these Whitehall decisions are the subject of complaints on the grounds of delay, bad decisions based on ignorance of local conditions, and lack of co-ordination between one decision and another. The Board of Trade has been strongly criticized for taking insufficient action to ensure a more balanced pattern of industrial development; 649 applications were made to its Advisory Committees in the period April 1960 to January 1963 for financial assistance under the Local Employment Act which was designed to encourage industrialists to set up factories in areas of high unemployment; but 306 were rejected.

There can be little doubt that Whitehall officials prefer to deal with 'national' or better still 'international' problems and tend to play off one local official or delegation against another. Lack of coordination can also lead to long delays, so that if a large housing estate may be built on the assurance that a new road is to be constructed, by the time the houses are completed the road may still be only on paper.

The trend towards regional government is already gathering momentum because it provides a solution to the problems of overgovernment at London and undergovernment in the provinces. Since the end of the last war the central government has been denuding the borough and the district councils of many functions – primary and secondary education, police and fire services, town and country planning, and some welfare services. Some of these functions have been transferred to the county councils, but they in turn have lost more powers than they have gained, including trunk roads, hospitals, municipal gas and electricity undertakings, and poor relief. The central government, however, has proceeded to administer these services not on a central but on a regional basis. For example, there are twelve area Electricity Boards, eleven area Gas Boards, and fourteen Regional Hospital Boards.

Responsibility for these regional boards rests with the Minister, who is usually too overworked to give much time to them. In fact they are more or less self-electing bodies. Is it any wonder that these bodies are generally regarded as the masters and not the servants of the people?

Recently the local authorities have been coming together in a regional framework with a view either to working out a regional plan, as in the case of the Standing Conference on London Regional Planning, or to achieving the benefits of large-scale organization, as in the C.L.A.S.P. and Yorkshire groups which have combined to exploit the advantages of mass-production orders for industrialized building systems.

The principal objection to regional government is that it might further denude local government of its powers. In fact local authorities and interests would participate more effectively if development plans were drawn up on a regional basis. In many cases, furthermore, the detailed work of day-to-day administration, for instance the management of primary and secondary schools, could best be done by the borough and district councils.

The question is not whether we move towards regional government but how we do so. The framework of local government is already breaking down on account of the weaknesses inherent in the system. Units are based on historical boundaries with no relation to size or efficiency. The Conservative Government more or less admitted this to be the case when it set up the Local Governments Commissions, but it only asked them to examine the boundaries and not the functions, and the reforms they have proposed only scratch at the problem. Even so, Rutland has proved too strong for Whitehall. What hope have we got of dealing, on this basis, with the problems posed by conurbations – decaying city centres, land scarcity, and congestion on the roads? The only answer is regional planning. Sir Geoffrey Crowther made this quite clear in the Steering Group's report on the Buchanan Report.

In the first stage the Regional Councils should be functional units drawing together all the departments, local authorities, and local interests. In the second stage the Regional Council should be directly elected, perhaps on the basis of one member for each parliamentary constituency. Only where the Regional Councils are directly elected will there be full participation of the people concerned. Only when regional loyalties replace provincial apathy will this country be back on the road towards a balanced Britain.

The regional department or planning authority would be a mixed-manned force at first, recruited from both inside and outside Whitehall. This would be a chance to get talented civil servants acquainted with the problems of industry and business. One reason for the failure of Whitehall to meet many of the postwar problems is undoubtedly the compartmentalism of British public life. Civil servants are recruited direct from universities and, once in Whitehall, get very few opportunities to acquire first-hand knowledge of industrial problems. The Regional Planning Authority would not only give top civil servants experience of practical problems but it would be a means of opening up a channel for recruitment into the Civil Service from industry and the professions, recruitment of men who had already proved themselves in regional government.

The scarcity of qualified people would make it necessary to bring in people with technical training. It would also be an opportunity to review Civil Service seniority provisions, pension arrangements, and salary differentials which at present restrict the freedom of movement between industry and government. One hesitates to recommend the establishment of yet another Royal Commission but the time has arrived for systematic and far-reaching reforms in the Civil Service itself. If these reforms were combined with proposals for the staffing of the regional planning authorities, it might be possible to graft on to the 'blind giant' of Whitehall some new limbs which in the future could play a perceptive role in public service.

3: Strategy for Growth

Economic growth above all depends on a willingness to accept change. Yet too many politicians on both the Right and the Left, who make glowing speeches about expansion, growth without inflation, and going straight ahead fast, are to be found in practice manning the barricades in defence of 'threatened' industries. In the same week as the Prime Minister made the announcement that Britain was applying to join the Common Market, the President of the Board of Trade announced that the Steel Company of Wales had been refused an application to import United States coal and would have to use instead the more expensive British fuel. In the same Budget speech as the Chancellor of the Exchequer appealed for a more competitive attitude of mind in British industry he imposed a tax on fuel oil so that industry could not take advantage of cheaper imported oil. Mr Wilson, at the time of the by-election in Dundee, told the House of Commons that he would take every step to expand trade with developing countries of the Commonwealth, and later in the same week wrote to the Labour candidate promising to continue to protect the uncompetitive Dundee jute industry (at the expense of Pakistan exports).

If we have not had a high rate of economic growth since the war then the blame must be put at the door of the two parties who while in government were reluctant to pay the price of change. Both Labour and the Tories are only too willing to pay over millions of pounds of public money to bolster up ailing industries. A classic example is the loan the Government was prepared to give Cunard to replace the Queens. The Government proposed, under its North Atlantic Shipping Act, to provide a loan of £14¾ million at the then current public works loan board rate of 6¼ per cent, and in addition an outright grant of £3¼ million. As the *Guardian* commented at the time: 'No business man would dream of putting his own money into an enterprise on the terms which the Government proposes for putting taxpayers' money into the building of a new Cunarder to replace the *Queen Mary*. ... The Government is taking 60 per cent of the risk in building the new liner while allowing the Cunard White Star Company to retain the whole of the equity interest in her.' Only the Liberals voted against the Bill. How long the electorate are willing to put up with this squandering of their money remains to be seen. An end to sops to inefficiency must come, however, if Britain is to achieve any worth-while system of economic planning and a high level of national investment. Too large a portion of our national investment has gone into projects such as the 1953 railway modernization plan and prestige liners.

A Competitive Economy

British industry, over a very wide field, has become remarkably uncompetitive since the war. A recent instance of this was provided by a detailed inquiry conducted for the National Incomes Commission and published in February 1964. This Report found that two months after the 5 per cent engineering wage settlement in December 1963 prices had risen in 'all sectors of business and the community'. The survey found that there was a definite 'price drift upwards', in some cases by twice as much as would have been justified on account of the wage award. The price increases extended far beyond the engineering industry. 'Time and time again products protected by strong trade associations were picked out for criticism as demanding a standard overall price increase with no real consideration of the costings or the productivity of the seller.' By the end of February 200 of the main grocery products had gone up in price.

Liberals would use anti-monopoly measures, make cuts in protective tariffs, and bring in tax reforms to ensure that firms convert a substantial part of the benefits of technical progress into lower prices instead of claiming the whole benefits for themselves, in higher profits and money wages. Rising money wages have not benefited the unions. They have had to fight hard to push weekly pay packets up from 160s. in 1951 to 311s. in 1962. But rising prices have meant that in real terms the increase in pay packets has only been 44 per cent in eleven years or $3\frac{1}{2}$ per cent per annum. Such were the workers' rewards under the Tory acquisitive society.

The employers have done much better. The rise in wages does

not worry them so long as they are able to pass on the increase to the consumer. What was important for them was the rise in the market value of their equity shares. Between 1951 and 1961 the market value of all securities quoted on the Stock Exchange has all but doubled. If capital was invested shrewdly in equity shares it was not difficult to treble capital values under the Tories. The very rich who owned property – particularly in Central London – were laughing. One professor has estimated that in the five years 1955–60 land values in Central London went up by 500 per cent. Is it any wonder that after twelve years of Conservative government 2.5 per cent of the adult population still owns 52.5 per cent of the personal wealth?

The Liberal party, representing the consumer rather than any vested interests, has always taken a strong line on monopolies. Once competitive conditions are established in industry it will not be so easy for manufacturers to put up their prices. Liberals would declare certain restrictive practices between companies illegal. Under the 1956 Restrictive Practices Act, all restrictive agreements had to be registered, but this piece of Conservative legislation has meant that only the most blatant price-fixing schemes have been condemned. Even members of these have little to fear, for the lawyers have devised what is called an open price agreement by which all the members 'inform' each other of prices and keep them in line. It is possible to break away from an 'open' price agreement but a variety of pressures are used by manufacturers, from control over distribution outlets and supplies to pressures inside trade associations to keep companies in line. In May 1963 the Select Committee on Nationalized Industries, reporting on the Electricity Supply Industry, said, for instance, that the manufacturers of transformers while observing the letter of the decision of the Restrictive Practices Court had flouted it in spirit by adopting a system of price leadership.

The comfortable network of restrictive practices encourages inefficiency throughout British industry. Why has more action not been taken by the Labour and Conservative governments to create a more competitive economy?

In Labour's case the whole idea of an open competitive economy clashes with the party's reluctance even to debate the restrictive practices which are maintained by some trade unions.

Competition, to the Labour party, is a 'jungle' which they abhor, preferring, as they do, controls and direction from Whitehall. The Conservative party is likewise reluctant to tread on the toes of its particular vested interests. In the Sudbury by-election Fisons, the fertilizer manufacturers, were revealed as significant contributors to Conservative party funds. Four years before in 1959 the Monopolies Commission reported that the price rings in the fertilizer industry were against the public interest. No action was taken by the Government. There is probably no connexion between the two facts. It would be better, however, if political contributions of this kind were not the main source of Conservative party funds.

There are many more Conservative backbenchers who have interests in trade associations and firms which indulge in restrictive practices. Sir Hugh Linstead, M.P., who has led the Conservative backbench revolt against the 1964 Restrictive Practices Bill, is also Secretary of the Pharmaceutical Society. It is an interesting sidelight on the power structure of the Conservative party that Mr Heath's Bill has created more opposition inside the Conservative Parliamentary Party than either Suez or the Profumo affair.

Liberals believe that resale price maintenance should be included on a list of banned practices. At the same time we maintain that action is required on a broad front against monopolies in general. To abolish R.P.M. without tackling monopolies is to leave the small efficient shopkeeper unprotected against unfair competition from large manufacturers and chain stores. The Liberal Parliamentary Party has proposed a 'fair trade charter' in the form of a series of amendments to the Resale Prices Bill. This charter would make it impossible for a supplier to give big discounts to one shop which he withheld from another. Similarly suppliers would not be able to run a 'give away' promotion scheme through one shop without giving it to all its competitors. It would also stop the practice of marking up goods in order to make 'fake cuts' afterwards.

If monopolies are to be dealt with in Britain the problem cannot be left to the courts. The responsibility must be with the government and with Parliament. The law courts are expert in deciding questions of fact but they should not be asked to make social and economic judgements with little guidance from the government. A new division of the Monopolies Commission should be empowered to scrutinize mergers; and recommendations already made by the Monopolies Commission which have not been carried out voluntarily should be enforced by a Board of Trade Order. Twenty-three out of the twenty-five reports of the Monopolies Commission have been made to Tory governments, and eighteen of them have called for action to end certain monopolies or restrictive practices. In only two cases have the Government made orders to put the recommendations into effect. Even when the most specific action was called for, as in the recommendation that Imperial Tobacco should sell its holding in Gallaghers, nothing was done. So long as this climate of opinion continues we must expect to see our share of the world export market continue to shrink and prices continue to rise.

Measures against monopolies and restrictive agreements are also vital to a successful incomes policy. Trade unions and their members cannot be expected to show restraint so long as monopolistic manufacturers are free to raise prices and profits when they please. If there were conditions of plant bargaining instead of national wage agreements (by which high and low productivity firms end up with the same basic wage award) it would be possible to relate wage increases to rises in productivity. The government could, after consultation with the unions and employers, fix annually a 'norm' and an appreciably higher 'ceiling' to wage increases in the light of the economic situation. Whereas the 'norm' would serve only as a guide to firms, the 'ceiling' would be enforceable and the government should insist that any firms which are earning more than enough to meet the 'ceiling' should pass on the benefits of their productivity to the consumer through lower prices.

Taxation

There is also a great need for radical changes in the tax system to encourage efficiency rather than tax avoidance. At present our tax system leans too heavily on earnings. A single man earning between £700 and £1,200, and a married man with three children earning £1,200–£1,900, were paying more direct taxes as a percentage of their incomes in 1961–2 than on the equivalent income in 1949–50. At the same time it has been possible to make enormous tax-free capital gains which are taxed only if security transactions are made twice in six months. The general body of taxpayers is also divided into the wealthy, who employ skilled men (who are engaged in a wholly unproductive battle with the Inland Revenue) and consequently know how to avoid paying the tax proportionate to their wealth, and those who are not so wealthy but pay tax at rates which are higher than they need be if the burden was fairly shared. A great deal of the existing tax avoidance rises from the complexity of the tax system. The Liberal Tax Committee's Report, which was hailed by Mr Douglas Houghton, M.P., the Labour Party Spokesman on tax matters, as 'the most significant outline of major tax reforms published in recent years', has shown how the tax system can be simplified, brought up to date, and made fairer by broadening the tax base and by removing the anomalies which create opportunities for exploiting avoidance devices. The report rejects the current fiction of a standard rate of tax which most taxpayers never pay and suggests that for the eight existing income tax schedules, surtax, and profits tax there should be substituted income tax on personal employment, business, and property, and a company tax. The report also recommends revolutionary proposals for taxing inherited wealth whether by way of gift or legacy and at rates according to the wealth of the recipient. This would encourage a wider distribution of wealth, and provide an equitable basis for any acceptable incomes policy.

Efficiency

Britain's low rate of productivity also stems from a failure to tap the full potential of our economic resources. A high level of demand is an essential element of faster economic growth. Government must therefore be organized in order that a long-term strategy for growth can be devised and implemented; but economic planning is not sufficient by itself. Productivity does not mean the same as production, although socialists often talk as if it does. It is concerned with not just how much you produce but also how efficiently you produce it, not only 'how big' but 'at what cost'. Output can increase without the same changes taking place in output per man-hour. In fact output can go up and at the same time productivity go down. A study of productivity in British industry* showed that, from 1948 to 1954, 31 out of 138 industries suffered a decline in productivity. In more than a third of these 31 industries output was rising all the time.

There can be little doubt that there is a good deal of dead wood in British industry. Even a Board of Trade sub-committee had to come to the following conclusion about the machine-tool industry in 1960: 'The first criticism is that the industry is too slow in its response to major rises in demand and that its delivery dates are too long and too unreliable.' The report also strongly criticized the industry for failing to innovate and modernize. 'U.K. imports are mainly high-performance and high-precision advanced types of special machine tools, while U.K. exports are mainly standard machine tools, many of them to the Commonwealth and the less highly industrialized countries.'

More recently, in July 1963, the Fielden Report has indicted the engineering industry. It points out that despite some notable exceptions too many British products are being out-classed in performance, reliability, and sales appeal. Whole sections of the engineering industry are out of date. This situation cannot be ignored. The engineering group of industries is responsible for half the United Kingdom's exports and 35 per cent of manufacturing industry's contribution to the national product. According to the report, much of the backwardness stems from the failure to recognize the importance of engineering design. The status of the designer is much too low. At present he is probably an apprentice who has worked his way up through night school and experience to the 'magnificent' salary of £1,000 a year.

This is only one symptom, however, of the low status of the whole engineering profession in British society. Recognition that a professional engineer needs education at university level has occurred only very recently. Out of the 870 new corporate members admitted to the Institution of Production Engineers in 1959 only 100 were university graduates. At that time nine tenths of the largest machine-tool firms in the country had only twenty-five graduate engineers amongst them.

The low status of the technologist is not confined to the

* R. J. Nicholson and S. Cynpta in the *Royal Statistical Society Journal*, 1960.

engineering industry. Over the broad field of British industry
the top is over-weighted with non-technical people. In Sweden,
for instance, 60 per cent of managing directors of scientific firms
hold degrees in science or engineering, whereas in England the
figure is only 12 per cent. Taking management as a whole the
university graduate is still in a minority. According to figures
quoted by David Granick in *The European Executive* only between a quarter and a third of top managers in British industry
are university graduates. By contrast in France, in large organizations, public and private, 40 per cent of the top executives
were found to be élite graduates of the Ecole Polytéchnique,
which provides a broad scientific education at the highest level.

British industry only reflects the class divisions in the country.
The combination of a sharply divided class society in the past
with the possibility of moving from one class to another through
business means has given the technician a second-class ticket
in the social pattern. The children of the successful entrepren-
eurs were sent to fashionable public schools and then into the
family business, the City, or the ancient universities where they
learnt that the place for the expert is in the back room where he
is 'on tap and not on top'.

It is quite clear that as a result there exists today a large number
of highly trained scientists and technologists who feel that their
talents are frustrated in industry and that Britain does not take
technology seriously enough.

What can be done to change this situation? The Liberal long-
run solution is education in its widest sense; less specialization
in school and undergraduate education which ensures that the
arts graduate can appreciate and discuss scientific problems with
the scientist, and vice versa. A high-level business school and
a broad advance towards the promotion of management studies
at technical colleges and C.A.T.s would also be major steps in
the right direction. On the other hand it must not be forgotten
that in 1948 an effort was made by Sir Stafford Cripps to give
management studies a boost. With his encouragement the
British Institute of Management was set up and courses established in the technical colleges leading to a National Certificate in
Management. But the Institute has never acquired significant
influence. The National Certificate courses have recently been

abandoned and the new Diploma in Management Studies started. Already this new award has come under severe criticism on account of the uncertainty of its subject content. British industry still believes that management – like industrial skills – can only be learnt 'on the job'. What is really required is a change of attitude on the part of those running our affairs.

So long as this situation continues Britain is likely to remain, to quote an American management consultant, Mr William W. Allen, 'a half-time country getting half-pay for half-work under half-hearted management'. Mr Allen in the *Sunday Times* of 1 March 1964 also drew attention to the degree to which there is considerable labour underemployment in British industry. He quotes the case of the Fawley refinery* where as a result of a productivity agreement it was possible to reduce the size of the work force since 1958 although a £23 million capital expansion programme had been completed in the meantime. If the productivity agreement had not been made Mr Allen estimates that the work force at the Fawley refinery would now be three times as large as that found in a similar North American refinery.

A Liberal Study Group on Employee Participation had previously drawn attention to the Fawley agreement, as one of the few instances in British industry 'where the scope for comprehensive and mutually profitable agreement between employers and unions has been matched by the vision and drive necessary to achieve it'. The agreement involved bargaining improvements in wages and working conditions against specific changes in working practices which were hampering the efficient use of labour. In February the management of the Fawley refinery presented the unions with an elaborate series of proposals for negotiation contained in a document known as the Blue Book. It offered unusually large increases in wage rates of around 40 per cent and a 40-hour week, in exchange for a number of changes in existing working practices. The major changes sought were drastic reductions of systematic overtime, the withdrawal of craftsmen's mates, and the relaxation of many job demarcations leading to inter-craft flexibility and the taking over of union maintenance jobs by process workers. Minor changes proposed were abolishing unproductive time allowances, simplifying wages

* Allan Flanders, *The Fawley Productivity Agreements*, Faber.

structure, and giving greater freedom to management in its use of supervision.

One of the conditions which facilitated the final agreements (which were the outcome of five months' difficult bargaining on the basis of the Blue Book) was the provision of a sufficiently large inducement which meant that even after the substantial overtime element in the weekly pay packets had been phased out employees were receiving higher wages. There were also safeguards as regards jobs and union security, the management gave a 'no-redundancy pledge', and the balance of crafts was preserved within the proposals for inter-craft flexibility. Even so, most of the sources of resistance had a security basis. Most important of all was the well-designed use of consultation at all levels, the greater part of which was informal and aimed at changing prevailing beliefs about the value of traditional or conventional practices.

The unions began by rejecting this all-or-nothing basis on which, as they saw it, the management was presenting the Book to them. All the craft unions, with the sole exception of the E.T.U., refused to accept the up-grading of craftsmen's mates and none of them would agree to union membership of the first-line supervisors becoming optional. On the remaining fourteen (out of sixteen) proposals, affecting maintenance and construction workers, agreement was found after various compromises.

The inter-craft flexibility items were whittled down to about half what the Blue Book had originally proposed. The T.G.W.U., which represented all non-craft, weekly paid employees, had to face the divergent attitudes of its shift- and day-work members, as the shift-workers stood to gain more by the proposals.

After agreement was reached in July 1960, overtime for maintenance and construction workers was successfully reduced in accordance with the phased targets, but there was less success in respect of process workers as there was not the same firm commitment. Among major changes in traditional practices, the withdrawal of mates and their redeployment was accomplished with few difficulties, but on the objective of greater flexibility in working practices, especially where these crossed union lines, limited progress was made. The agreements led to increasing formality in union–management relations, while within the unions they have led to a much closer overlap in the functions of shop stewards and union officials. The underlying problem, of the extent to which traditional job territories can be preserved in the light of technical changes, has remained unaffected by the agreements.

In 1962 management at Fawley wanted to continue its departure from conventional collective bargaining and it produced an Orange Book offering wage increases in return for union acceptance of a further list of changes, mainly in job demarcations and duties. This was designed as a second instalment of productivity through greater flexibility. The unions put in counterclaims based on the cost of living and comparability, and after protracted negotiations, agreements were reached with the T.G.W.U. and the craft unions. The Orange Book was abandoned in favour of joint management-union committee to work out agreed suggestions for three groups: the craftsmen, and the day and shift branches of the T.G.W.U. These committees showed more positive acceptance by the union officials of the day T.G.W.U. branch, but among craftsmen there was considerable resistance to extending inter-craft flexibility.

The Liberal policy for industrial relations would create the right environment for the negotiation of similar productivity agreements. So long as there are inadequate, or the complete absence of, redundancy benefits, workers and unions must be expected to fight shy of change and the reduction of overtime working. Why should workers change unless they have some firm assurances that they will benefit from the new arrangements?

Industry-wide bargaining means that change takes place only as fast as the least efficient employer and the least competent trade unionist permits it to proceed. And change is possible only if there is a sense of partnership rather than an atmosphere of struggle in British industrial relations.

The evidence of underemployment in British industry is considerable. Statistics collected by the Industrial Labour Office for the last year show that Australia, Austria, Canada, France, West Germany, Norway, and Switzerland all work fewer hours in manufacturing industry than the British average of forty-six hours a week. In New York, in 1963, electricians have been doing a week's work in twenty-five hours with up to five hours' permitted overtime under an agreement negotiated by the International Brotherhood of Electrical Workers.

Comparisons of British and American productivity for individual industries prepared by Cambridge University and the O.E.E.C. in 1959 point out that U.S. output per worker in 1950 was higher in different sectors. In the distributive trades the average U.S. worker's output was nearly twice that of the average British worker. In agriculture it was nearly twice as big; in manufacturing generally nearly 3 times as big; in transport and communications over 4 times; in the fuel industries over $7\frac{1}{2}$ times. Within manufacturing industry it was found that the American superiority was most marked in industry when there is scope for mechanization and automation of processes and where the labour share in the total product is correspondingly high, such as metal cans, automobiles, trucks and tractors, agricultural machinery, radios, and basic industrial chemicals.

These products are among those which show the fastest rate of growth in international trade. Now as Professor Barna has pointed out in *The Times* of 4 April 1963: 'The shortfall in British net exports of manufactures compared with either the United States or Western Germany can be entirely accounted for by the shortfall in the fastest growing machinery and chemical products. In all other manufactures, taken together, Britain's position is at least as good as theirs. ... The inferior trading position of Britain is thus an indication of technical backwardness. While cost elements such as the level of wages are important for the older type of product (e.g. ships or locomotives) trade in the newer types tends to be influenced largely by availability. The more closely one looks at international trade the more evident this becomes. Britain's position is worse in electric than in non-electric typewriters and worse in the latest than in other vintages of plastics.'

The State and Development

It is well known that Britain is not only lagging behind its industrial competitors in many fields of scientific research, but that we have failed to put into application and large-scale production many of the fundamental discoveries which have been

T—B

made in this country. Major examples of fundamental research being done in Britain but put into large-scale production by American companies first are penicillin, fluorescent lighting, computers, and silicone. The result is that we are losing our share of the world market for manufactured goods.

The National Institute for Economic and Social Research has pointed out in the May 1962 issue of *Economic Review* that, after adjusting the exchange rate to get a comparison which is as near as possible in real terms, it seems that American industry's research and development expenditure is over five times as large as British industry's absolute figure: it is nearly three times as large per employee and twice as large as a percentage of net output. Unfortunately separate comparisons are not made for research and for development but there can be little doubt that international comparison for development alone would be even more disadvantageous to this country.

Mr Wilson's answer to this problem is that the government, not industry, should decide what is worth developing, and then pump millions of pounds into the projects through research and development contracts. But he admitted in the same speech that 'we have spent thousands of millions in the past few years on misdirected research and development contracts in the field of defence'. The conclusion he drew in his very next sentence was: 'If we were now to use the technique of R. and D. contracts in civil industry I believe we could, within a reasonable period of time, establish new industries that would make us once again one of the foremost industrial nations of the world.' In other words, having wasted thousands of millions of public money because civil servants were unable to assess the advantage or otherwise of defence projects, we should now apply the same techniques to the rest of British industry.

Mr Wilson's faith in the wisdom of the government's dictating research targets is not shared by the officials of the National Research Development Corporation (the body which the Labour Programme, *Signposts for the Sixties,* singled out as the agency for greater public support for research and development). In an article in the *National Provincial Bank Review* for August 1963 it has been made quite clear by two officials of the N.R.D.C. that in the experience of their organization research and development is most fruitful when carried out by industry.

The best place for research and development is industry because a high-grade and expanding industry should presumably know what it wants and where the opportunities for growth and profits are, and should have the technological and commercial expertise to make the appropriate valuations. Except in the field of defence and other public requirements, it is doubtful if the Government can or should try to dictate what research targets should be. ... During the period 1949 to 1962 all such public organizations (government research establishments, universities, and other corporate institutions) communicated about 5,600 inventions to N.R.D.C. The overwhelming proportion of these derived from scientifically trained personnel who believed that their inventions had commercial prospects. Yet only 5 per cent actually became royalty revenue earners, that is, were turned into established industrial products.

The Labour leaders do not seem to realize that there are always far more research ideas than can be put into practice. The greatest obstacle to innovation is not the lack of ideas, but the risk inherent in developing and establishing a new process, product, or device. As well as overcoming the technical development difficulties a new enterprise faces considerable commercial risks. The new product may have become obsolete by the time it is fully developed. Mr Wilson actually seems to believe that he can 'persuade' industry to accept the risks involved in development of an innovation if he adds the bait of state control! That is what he said at Scarborough at the 1963 Labour Conference: 'where new industries are established on the basis of State-sponsored research, the State will control the industries which result'.

Liberals believe that industry should be helped over the 'development hump' by public bodies like the N.R.D.C., whose capital they would like to see increased, but unlike the Socialists they consider that this can be achieved only through persuading industry that partnership in a venture is worth while and that if the project succeeds the industry (including the employees) will reap attractive profits. If the company did not think it was going to be profitable there would be no public money available.

There is no reason to be dogmatic about the way the State should share in the profits. If the State takes an equity-type risk

in financing a new project it should expect to receive appreciation on its shareholding as well as a dividend. On the other hand,
unlike the Labour party which wants to control industry, Liberals believe that it is not the task of government to run industry
and therefore consider that industry should have a chance to
buy back the State's shares at a later stage. In other cases the
State might receive payment in the form of royalties. Where a
new product was of considerable interest to a number of firms or
industries but not sufficiently so for any one to take a vigorous
lead, the State should be prepared to act as a catalyst; in this
case there would be grounds for public funds being used for
equity financing of a joint consortium.

Liberals would also encourage industry to make more use of
fewer research associations. At present more than half the
fifty-odd research associations have a total income of £100,000
each – far less than the average research development expenditure of a large British firm. Only nine research associations have
incomes greater than £250,000 a year, and not one of them has
an income even half as big as the average research and development expediture of a large American firm. Clearly most of
them do not dispose of adequate resources for development
work and consequently their share of total industrial research
and development has been declining. Yet it is only through joint
effort in research and development that this country can hope to
equal the economies of large-scale research and development
possible in America, Russia, and, now, the Common Market.

More needs to be done to help the small and medium-sized
companies. There are at least 50,000 small firms (employing less
than 250 employees) and 3,000 medium-sized firms (between
250 and 500 employees). Although the small and medium-sized
companies employ more than half of all the employees in manufacturing industry, there is less than one qualified employee
for each three firms. The small and medium-sized companies
have had some remarkable successes in the field of innovations.
The major non-mechanical advance in the textile industry in the
inter-war period was the discovery in 1929 of a method of ren-
dering cotton and viscose fabrics resistant to creasing. The whole
textile industry knew of the possibility but the discovery was
made in the research laboratory of a medium-sized company –

Tootal Broadhurst Ltd – by a relatively small team of research workers.

Similarly, the first regular system of high definition TV. in the world was set up in the U.K. in 1935 as a result of the work done by a small team at E.M.I., which was then a much smaller company than many others engaged in the development of TV. These are only two examples of the innovations which were not only made but developed by small or medium-sized British companies; the same may also be said of improvements in insulin, air-conditioning equipment, automatic transmission, power steering, magnetic recording, and synthetic detergents, which have not for the most part been the work of large industrial laboratories.

In the present shortage of scientists little can be done for smaller firms without diverting qualified men from equally or more important tasks such as basic research or teaching. Some general recognition, however, of the fundamental value of scientists and scientific work to the country should be given through the taxation system, and it is suggested that a tax incentive be given on the salaries of qualified scientists engaged on scientific work. This incentive could be framed to benefit the smaller firm only, e.g. by raising the profits tax abatement limit upwards from £12,000, or to benefit all firms by introducing an investment allowance on such salaries. The rate of incentive need not be high or costly (for instance an investment allowance of $2\frac{1}{2}$ per cent might cost no more than £3 millions in tax revenue); but the mere existence of such a differential showing the material importance of science would be of enormous value. On logical grounds, moreover, such an incentive would be far more defensible than the present indiscriminating investment allowance given on all purchases of new plant.

Economic Planning

A great deal of investment made by the government and British industry since the war has also been misdirected. Too much money has been invested in the wrong direction because there has been insufficient information about the economy and the targets required for a rapid rate of growth. The people who direct our affairs in Whitehall and industry are often ill equipped to make the right decisions. What we need is better and more sophisticated economic planning.

All three parties, today, subscribe to economic planning. Liberals differ from Labour in so far as the latter tend to treat the word 'planning' as an incantation which will solve all problems. Furthermore Liberals consider the essential contribution of government to economic planning is the central coordination of forecasts and targets which are made in the different parts of the economy. Labour seems to regard planning as a means by which the State transmits its ideas about rates of growth to industry rather than the other way round. Mr Wilson thinks in terms of the State deciding in advance which industries would 'deserve' a higher investment allowance or some other discriminating form of taxation. Liberals do not believe that the State should get involved in this kind of judgement. Obviously, if the machine-tool industry is working on a lower estimate than the motor industry about the likely demand for cars in the future, the result will be a bottleneck. If the government has put the different forecasts of industry into a consistent picture, however, and related the situation to a national rate of growth and a rising level of demand, it seems likely that most industries would fit in with the government's policy. They would have to have good reasons for doing anything else because if their expectations were lower than the actual rate achieved they would miss out on considerable profits.

Liberals differ from Conservatives about the priority they would give to economic growth over all other economic priorities. The country's crisis of confidence can be resolved only if industry and the people are convinced that expansion will continue at a steady rate of growth. At present, however, the National Economic Development Council is only an advisory body. Executive decisions in economic affairs are still made by the Treasury and the Chancellor of the Exchequer. Recently Conservative Chancellors have put much greater emphasis on economic expansion. Their words have not always been borne out by events. In 1962 Mr Selwyn Lloyd announced that 'the theme of the Budget is the maintenance of a firm lease for sound expansion'. During the next twelve months the gross domestic product declined by $\frac{1}{2}$ per cent.

The concentration of power in the Civil Service in one single department, the Treasury, has created major problems in the field of economic policy. For the Treasury is not only responsible for economic planning and policy making; it is the controller of the spending policies of other departments, as well as the administrative heart of the Civil Service concerned with the various departments' staffing, pay, and expenditure. When this is said it is easy to understand how the Treasury has developed a tradition of introversion in Whitehall. Cut off, itself, from other departments by reason of its position as the unit in charge of personnel management and promotion, its main task has been to bludgeon the other departments each year into some sort of annual budget. It was Harold Laski who pointed out that 'it is a grave administrative mistake to concentrate this massive power of negation in the hands of, relatively, a small number of officials who have no other function but the forthright utterance of the Everlasting Nay'.

Yet this was the department which, until the setting up of Neddy, was also responsible for discharging such economic growth policy-making as was carried out by the Government. It is the carry-over, into the general field of economic affairs, of the same method of control through cutting down of expenditure which created the infamous Treasury view 'when in doubt, deflate'. This is, of course, only part of the story. The Treasury, during most of the post-war years, has given a higher priority to maintaining sterling as an international currency than it gave to economic expansion. This delusion of grandeur appealed to the Treasury men. 'No species in Whitehall', points out Anthony Sampson, 'is more distinct than the Treasury Men, for they are the mandarins among mandarins.' The Treasury lack of understanding of the outside would not be helped by the fact that it has only one scientist and fewer than two dozen economists, and most of these are on short-service engagements. It is little wonder that scientists angrily complain that their projects are turned down by committees without a single scientist, and they counter-attack by making outrageous demands for money, knowing that they will be cut by half but finding them sometimes suddenly accepted.

It might be thought that the setting up of the N.E.D.C. and

the recent internal reforms in the Treasury would have gone far to solve these problems. The Treasury was reconstructed in 1962. The Head of the Civil Service, who until that time was, almost unbelievably, expected to be not only in charge of the management side of the Civil Service, but also Secretary to the Cabinet, was relieved of the latter duties. The other half of the Treasury – the economic and financial side – was divided into 'three groups': the first responsible for finance, which includes management of money at home and overseas; the second, for the Public Sector, which includes not only many Whitehall departments and nationalized industries, but also Covent Garden Opera, the National Theatre, and the Art Galleries; and a third group the national Economy Division, which is the head of the economic policy side of the Treasury. It is concerned with the operations of the other departments not as spenders but as contributors to economic policy. It also deals with N.E.D.C. and is responsible for forecasting and coordinating the Government's income policy.

It would be far more valuable if the latter group, responsible for the National Economy, should be hewn off from the rest of the Treasury and formed into a new Ministry known as either Economic Affairs or the Ministry of Expansion. This would not only help to overcome some of the problems which arise from over-centralization in Whitehall, it would also give the planning unit of government a well-defined place in the administrative structure. At present N.E.D.C. is producing tentative policy proposals through which a five-year plan can be implemented in the U.K. However, they are still subject to Treasury scrutiny. There is no guarantee that proposals formulated by N.E.D.C. in consultation with the outside world will be able to get the seal of approval from the more monastic officials of the National Economy Group in the Treasury. Only when a proper Ministry of Economic Affairs is set up and injected with the enthusiastic new blood of the N.E.D.C. will a grand strategy for the British economy be evolved and carried out.

More fundamental still is the objection to a fine-spun system of controls (which will have to be evolved if all policy is to fit into a forecast and a plan for the development of the whole economy of Britain) being devised and implemented by a body which is not under democratic control. It does not seem to concern Conservatives that the secretariat of N.E.D.C. is responsible, not to Parliament, but to a council of employers and trade unions. The problem probably does not even arise. After all they have always thought in terms of an economic world inhabited not by people, or even consumers, but by organized labour and employer federations, in just the same way as they think in outdated political terms of a two-party system consisting of a Labour party representing the workers and the Conservatives representing the salaried and people of independent means.

As a matter of fact Britain is today a rather closely regulated society. We are not free to spend the majority of our earnings as we wish. There are subtantial amounts deducted in tax before we even receive our wages or salaries. Employers are not free to negotiate individually with their workers. It is not possible to practise certain trades or professions, no matter how qualified one is, if the antiquated apprenticeships have not been served. Shopkeepers cannot keep their shops open when they wish. One cannot build a house where one wants. Many of the traditional liberties have already been eroded by the controls of organized society.

Liberals are not appalled by this – but do believe the planners should be under democratic control. At first some Liberals were concerned lest the eating away of individual liberties by the planned interve tion of the State would destroy the basic liberties for which Liberals have always fought. Now intervention by Government is accepted on a wide front because most people are today freer and not less free in the welfare state. There are two basic reasons for this state of affairs. The infringements of individual liberty are not haphazard but are implemented by rules laid down by legislation and collective agreements. Consequently the erosions of liberty of action are themselves under the control of the democratic process. They can be changed and do change according to public opinion and the efficiency of the democratic machinery in translating this opinion into governmental action.

Secondly, the welfare state had been an economic as well as a social success. The present level of taxation would have been completely unacceptable at the beginning of the century or even before the Second World War. People today, however, have become accustomed to high rates of taxation, which they now find bearable because they associate high government spending with high standards of living.

Liberals have played no small part in this social revolution. It was the Liberal Government of 1906–14 which laid the foundations for the existing welfare state by introducing old-age pensions, unemployment insurance, and health insurance. It also introduced graded income tax, surtax and estate duty, the system of redistributory taxation which raises the money to pay for social advance. At that time too, Liberals introduced the first Town and Country Planning Act and the Coal Mines Wages Act – the first State guarantee of a minimum wage. Of eighteen factory Acts since 1833, Liberals have been responsible for twelve.*

Planned intervention by the State, therefore, is acceptable to Liberals so long as it is open to democratic control and so long as it is concerned with created conditions in which the individual can develop his personality to the full. Recent years have been characterized by a growing sense of frustration, however, rather than any feeling of participation. The fact is that for most of the electorate steady growth is not just a desirable policy: it is an economic necessity. This is why Liberals want to give overriding authority in the economic field to a Ministry of Expansion which would be responsible for drawing up a five-year plan; this would be debated and amended by Parliament – not N.E.D.C. – and then implemented at the national level by the various ministries concerned and regionally by the regional planning authorities.

There is a grave danger, however, that, unless a radical party is built up in the next few years, Britain will be unable to sustain high and prolonged economic growth. As we have seen, economic growth depends on a willingness to accept change and on the quality of the people who direct our economy both in Whitehall and in industry. Britain's slow rate of economic growth since the war is a reflection of the fact that the Government has not responded to the needs of the new men – the technicians, the

* Desmond Banks, *Liberals and Economic Planning* (Unservile State Papers No. 8, Liberal Publications Dept).

junior executives, the teachers, and the scientists – who are the mainspring of economic growth in a modern society.

Economic expansion is not one among many policy objectives to the young executive – it is a political necessity. His life is directly affected by a credit squeeze. When the Bank Rate goes up to penal levels and the government sends out directives to the banks asking for a 'curtailment of credit facilities', he has no possibility of getting a loan. So he has to go to H.P. finance companies, which involves actual rates of interest of anything from 12 to 15 per cent. Mortgage rates also go up with the credit squeeze, and building society loans become not only much more expensive but also scarcer. At the same time the price of housing actually seems to go up just as fast, if not more rapidly, in times of credit squeeze, which can stop all municipal building and slow down private building in an area.

Reorganization

This deep sense of frustration arises from the realization on the part of the new men that modern life has a great deal to offer. It also arises from a feeling of exclusion from any real decision-making or responsibility in the running of our national affairs. The young executive was not just 'letting off steam', as Mr Macmillan described it, when at Orpington he overturned a Tory majority of 14,760 into a Liberal majority of 7,855. The New Men find themselves frustrated and challenged at every turn, not only by the Whitehall machine, but by the established interest groups and the sheer impersonality of modern industrial organization. They recognize that the Liberal party's proposals for economic growth and change would go a long way to remove the obstacles in the road of progress and democratic participation.

First, reorganization of central government and the setting up of a new Ministry for Economic Affairs would give an opportunity for better communications between the New Men and Whitehall. At present the underlying assumption seems to be that the real business of government is none of the public's business. Yet it is an essential ingredient of a mass society that people are able to understand where the government is going. Not only would much greater explicitness help the executives and the shop stewards to know what was happening but it would also make people more responsive to rapidly changing needs.

Second, the implementation of growth targets through regional plans would give the New Men direct participation in the actual process of development. One of the most successful features of the French Plan has been the way in which thousands of local leaders drawn from industry, trade unions, and consumer groups have played a key role in the implementation as well as the construction of the targeting. It could be argued that this will be achieved in Britain through the proposed regional Neddies. However, these are open to the same criticism as a national Neddy if it is the central planning authority. Moreover, it would lead only to greater frustration if the proposals of the regional Neddies are not taken up and acted on.

In any case, industrial development cannot be conceived at the regional level except in the context of development plans for transport, housing, and industrial training and education. Consequently it is essential that industrial planning is carried out in coordination with other aspects of development planning done by regional planning authorities. Both aspects of planning must be carried out by the same authority and must be responsible eventually to a directly elected regional council. Of course the regional planning authorities would want to consult both the management and the trade-union leaders, both regarding the drawing up of the regional plans and concerning their execution. If it was found that councils composed of industrialists, union leaders, and local interests were the best way to achieve maximum consultation, then it might be desirable to continue the N.E.D.C. councils at both regional and national levels, as consultative bodies. On the whole, however, it would seem that this role should be left to the elected council at the regional level and Parliament on questions of national interest. It is a sad reflection on the state of industrial relations if the government can achieve trade-union participation in economic planning only by offering a *quid pro quo* from the management side. Liberals do not believe that this need be so and have specific proposals for improving industrial relations which will be discussed in a later chapter.

It is no use pretending that anything short of major surgery is going to prevent regional unemployment getting worse. A completely new approach to industrial development is needed. The Government is now trying to graft on to the development policy of the Local Employment Act a regional policy for north-east England and the Central Lowlands of Scotland. But the Local Employment Act is based on a mistaken idea that government can solve the question of regional unbalance by merely mopping up unemployment in penny packets. The Act provides that any area where a high rate of unemployment exists should be called a development district. The areas as designated under the Act were too small, however, and as they often consisted of economic black-spots no one wanted to go there anyway. Lord Eccles, who ought to know, as he introduced the Act as President of the Board of Trade, admitted as much in the House of Lords on 28 November 1962. 'My Lords,' he said, 'I have a confession to make. I have changed my mind since I had in the Board of Trade to do with the Local Employment Bill. I used then to think that we should develop a kind of rescue service which would deal with all the persistent patches of local unemployment, large and small, wherever they occurred. I now see that the time has passed for encouraging minor developments which put a district more or less at the mercy of one method of production, or of demand for one kind of goods. Technical change has become too rapid and too rough to take risks of that kind with small communities. We need something more radical and something long-sighted.'

Liberal development strategy would not be based on pouring sand into the gaps in the dyke, as at present, but on fostering new industrial growth points in each of the major regions which are at present lagging behind south-east England. In spite of Liberal amendments to the Finance Act 1963, advocating the establishment of economic growth points which would tap the unemployment of traditional black spots, the Chancellor of the Exchequer saw fit to restrict the increased grants and the more rapid write-off permitted under the 1963 Budget to areas designated by the abortive Local Employment Act as development districts. Perversely the Government has incorporated the concept of growth points on a limited scale in the regional plans for north-east England and central Scotland. But growth points to be effective must be part of a national strategy devised on the basis of providing an alternative to the drift to the south-east. As long as Whitehall is not concerning itself with overall policy considerations of this kind, drift will continue. Furthermore, any regional plan will be inadequate unless it is based on targets related to a national plan. The Government has been completely unable to devise any adequate economic targets for either the north-east or central Scotland. This was made obvious in the Government White Paper for north-east England, which stated that it was hoped that emigration from the region could be reduced from 4,000 to 2,500 as a result of the plan. Without any national plan it is quite impossible to decide whether this figure is adequate or inadequate, as it can be judged only on an estimate of what the other regions could absorb – which will not be known until industrial development is implemented through a series of regional economic plans on the basis of a national strategy for growth.

4: The New Face of Britain

Counterdrift

If we go on as we are the physical face of Britain could be ruined by the end of the century. Cities are continuing to spread outwards while their centres decay. The growth of population alone will require that the equivalent of forty new cities the size of Bristol are built. Should the drift to the south go on for the next forty years, there will be conditions of almost unbroken conurbation stretching from Dover to Bristol and as far north as Lancashire and Yorkshire. To this enormous building programme must be added the task of rebuilding our decaying city centres. Slums at present are growing twice as quickly as they are cleared. In England and Wales alone there are still some 3¾ million dwellings which were built before the Public Health Act of 1875, that is before there were any official minimum standards of building construction. Meanwhile the roads have already become so congested that traffic in many towns has been reduced to a crawl. What will happen by the end of the century? According to Professor Buchanan, allowing for the increase in population, there could be a grand total of 40m. motor vehicles by the year 2000. Already Britain has more motor vehicles per mile of road than any other country in the world. At the existing rate of motorway construction we should just about have completed the first 1,000 miles target (which Mr Marples promised by 1970) by the end of the century, and by that time there could be 40,000 vehicles per mile of motorway.

In the countryside many of our small country towns and villages are rapidly losing their population and their vitality. Within six miles of the centre of Oxford, probably one of the most prosperous cities in England, it is possible to find decaying and abandoned houses. In certain areas such as North Wales and the Scottish Highlands and Islands, whole regions are in desperate need of rejuvenation. The result is that in the south-east of England in many areas only two or three years' supply of building land remains, and housing land prices have reached over £12,000 per acre in Kent and Essex; whereas similar land is still available in Yorkshire and elsewhere in the north for less than £2,100.

These problems will have to be given immediate attention by any government. They cannot be solved in isolation; each is interrelated, and to tackle any one of them on its own would be not only insufficient but also ineffective. That is why a high-level unit – call it a Ministry of Regional Development – must be set up in Whitehall to produce a fully comprehensive national policy relating to the location of population and employment in Britain. This high-level unit should not be a vast bureaucratic Ministry concerned with drawing up a blueprint for Britain in which there would be a slot or a number for everyone. This is perhaps a Labour vision of Britain. It is certainly not a Liberal one. What is needed in Whitehall is a strategy rather than detailed planning. All too often in recent years the impression has been given that the various government ministries each go their own way with very little reference to one another. The Board of Trade was encouraging industry to move into Liverpool at the same time as the Ministry of Housing and Local Government was trying to get people to move out of Merseyside. Similarly the present road construction programme of the Ministry of Transport is being carried out without full regard for the locational problems created by the new investment.

The first priority in the strategy for Regional Development should be to set in motion a counterdrift policy. This policy should be designed to create a series of related growth points or city regions in order that a balance can be maintained between the different regions of Britain. If this is not done, by the end of the century there will be twice as many people per square mile in the south-east of England as there are in the Netherlands today. On the other hand large parts of the north of England and the West Country will be quite sparsely populated.

A national policy will also have to consider whether the new population will want to be diffused over large areas in low-density housing with regional shopping centres on the American pattern, or whether the new population centres should be more compact and set in open country. This question cannot be separated from the problem of counterdrift. It is not possible to decide whether a high or low population density should be encouraged until it has been determined whether forty new towns the size of Bristol or eight new conurbations the size of Birmingham would provide a more effective counterbalance to the attractions of the existing London–Manchester axis.

In fact the choice would probably be a conurbation of both high and low density having as much diversity as possible. This would be the Liberal aim. If the drift to the south-east continues, however, the result will be an appalling uniformity of suburban sprawl over southern England with more people living under city conditions than there are people living in the whole of Britain today.

Planning by Regions

The alternative is to build a series of linked regional centres. The nucleus of these would be existing centres such as Carlisle or Bristol. Around these centres, which would probably be developed on a high-density basis, would be a ring of new towns designed as all-purpose developments, which would combine facilities for living and working. At present, by contrast, the New Towns have been built so close to London that they might well be considered urban sprawl which has jumped the Green Belt. Similarly the New Towns of Glasgow are so near the city that they are virtually little more than planned suburbs.

The siting of these clusters of New Towns would be the responsibility of the regional planning authorities. The region is the proper unit for planning the social and economic aspects of development and for determining the proper course for urban growth and redevelopment. Local planning authorities have a major role to play but it is essential that their policies should be coordinated and that they should work together towards a co-ordinated goal. This goal must give top priority to human welfare. The needs of the people of north-west England are altogether different from south-east England, and with the best will in the world a Ministry in London cannot fully appreciate a regional problem.

Each regional planning authority would consider those particular problems which need to be looked at over the region as a whole – the location of industry, the availability of land for development both for housing and other purposes, the designation and preservation of green belts or green wedges, and the need for urban development. Each authority should have before it a budget, drawn up in consultation with the Ministry, of the resources which can be made available for improving its particular region. The way in which these resources are used, however, should, within broad limits, be the responsibility of the regional authority. Regional drive and initiative will depend in the long run on the individual interest of the local men and women, not just the local big-wigs but ordinary people who care about the surroundings and amenities in which they live. Once people feel that they can play a part in determining the shape of their own locality we shall get some new blood and interest in town and country planning. So long as local government is concerned largely with refuse disposal, and 'planning' is a remote bureacratic function operated from Whitehall, the resignation of the ordinary person to the squalor of his surroundings will continue.

Public interest and participation in redevelopment must be strengthened. The regional councils, in conjunction with the local authorities, must encourage inhabitants of a street to get together, as they have been doing in many places, and take advantage of what modern life has to offer in making our surroundings brighter, safer, and more beautiful. Local community associations should be brought into the process of planning. Too often these are only set up to preserve the *status quo*. They would also be encouraged to get residents together to discuss the ways in which their own particular area can be improved.

No region will ever respond to government initiative unless it feels the spur of responsibility. Yet this is what the government has so far avoided doing. As a *Times* leader of 15 November 1963 pointed out: 'one aspect of the White Papers which might be serious is that the regions remain largely paper concepts, no real concrete expression of regional unity is proposed, beyond the single building in Newcastle in which the regional representatives of key Whitehall departments will all have their offices.' This is not enough. Not only must the regional plan be the responsibility of those living in these parts but they must also have a strong voice in how the money is spent and the resources allocated. This raises the complex subject of local government finance. The present rating system is both unfair and inadequate for the purpose of regional government. It takes no account of a person's ability to pay. The system imposes a penalty upon improvement and provides no incentive for development or redevelopment. Further, more rating is regressive in character as it tends to fall more heavily upon those with low incomes, and it is, for this reason, limited in potential.

Local Finance

The whole system of local finance needs to be completely over-hauled also. In particular site-value rating would have advantages over the existing system because it would encourage development rather than act as a deterrent. If an improvement was made to the building or house, the valuation on which the rates would be assessed would not be changed. Under the present system an improvement entails higher rates so that the individual is penalized for improving his own property. Taxing the land and not the development would also allow the community to share in increased land values arising from redevelopment. It would also encourage land which had development possibilities to be brought into the market.

At present developers buy up land as a speculation and, although development permission has been granted, they sit on the land and wait for the prices to rise. Under a system of site-value rating the building land would be rated and developers would have strong incentives to develop the site as quickly as possible. Building land where no development has taken place would be rated at a higher level than other land, in order to discourage land hoarding. This would be particularly appropriate in regions where new cities in the form of clusters of new towns were to be encouraged. A great deal of public expenditure in the form of infrastructure investment in housing, schools, roads, public utilities, community centres, and industrial estates would be necessary before self-sustained growth could be triggered off in these developments. A family of urban projects might well require expenditure over five years of £50 to £100 millions. These pace-making projects, however, will attract further expenditure from industrial and commercial concerns which would, in turn, lead to rising land prices. If the region could recoup its expenditure over the years by taxing these rising land values it could tap a source of increasing wealth in the same way as the State shares in the rise in national income through income tax. This land taxation could be progressive (as in income tax) so that the owner-occupier would be paying a much smaller percentage rate of the valuation of the land he occupies than the commercial developer who owns the expansive site in the city centre or suburban shopping centre. It could be assessed quinquennially, but paid annually. One of the by-products of this new assessment would be a system of regional land registration. This, in itself, would speed up the process of town and country planning. At present the planners do not know who owns which piece of land. It would also provide a check that capital gains made on land transactions were paid, as the registrar would have to be informed when land had changed hands and what price was paid.

Land-Ownership

The rejuvenation of the older industrial cities requires extensive urban renewal. Most of the slum blackspots are found in the north of England, the Midlands, Scotland, or south Wales. In England and Wales, for instance, there are fifty blackspots, but all but five of these areas are in the north or the Midlands. This will be another very costly affair. Plans recently announced by Glasgow Corporation estimate that the rebuilding of one slum district, the Cowdaddens, will cost between £40 and £50 million. Finance is one of the two fundamental problems associated with urban renewal. The second is the problem of securing comprehensive rather than piecemeal development.

If our cities are to be rebuilt comprehensively and to be designed as a whole, unified land-ownership is imperative. The Labour party answer to this problem is land nationalization. They propose the establishment of a National Land Commission which would take into public ownership the freehold of all land upon which building or rebuilding is to take place. But this would hinder rather than speed up development. Since the would-be developer would automatically lose his freehold by building on his own land, it is more likely that he would simply sit tight under a Labour Government and hope for better days at the next General Election. Indeed, he would have nothing to gain and much to lose by selling his freehold to the National

Land Commission, for not only would he lose his freehold but he would also receive payment for it at less than its true market value (i.e. mainly on existing use value). The only way in which the Labour party could then prevent a drastic decline in the rate of development would be to resort to the massive use of compulsory purchase orders which, in effect, would be tantamount to land nationalization. Small wonder that the Report of the Committee appointed by the Civic Trust and published in June 1962 under the title *Urban Redevelopment* declared that 'the prospect of *ad hoc* nationalization would discourage private development'. Not only is this the case, but implicit in the Labour party's analysis is the assumption that the State would always be able to gauge better than the developer for what purpose the public would like to use the property.

But it is quite unnecessary for a public authority to buy up at once *all* land capable of development. It would be enormously expensive; and it might well retard overall development, for private enterprise is already doing some valuable work. Where no drastic change in the road pattern or land use is necessary, private developers can play a most valuable role. The important job is to tackle the urban areas which demand changes of a more radical nature. Where the street layout is often completely out of date and unsuited to the motor age, it will not be possible to make far-reaching changes in the size and shape of sites so long as a large number of individual owners each rebuild their own plots.

By far the most helpful step would be to set up a Land Development Corporation which would make available loans to the regional councils on a deferred interest basis, so that land could be compulsorily acquired at a price based, as at present, on current market value. It would be resold, however, at a price which reflected any change in its value resulting from the use prescribed for it in the new scheme. Until the land was resold, the loan charges on the cost of acquiring it would be carried by the Corporation as an accumulated deficit. This arrangement would have several advantages. It would bridge the financial gap between purchase and disposal without overburdening the rates, for although these would be supplemented by the land tax most of the urban renewal is required in areas where land values are lower than in the more congested south. Furthermore it would soon become a revolving fund, for all the areas need not be taken over at once, and as they were sold for development the fund would get its money back. It would, however, allow any profits made on the resale of sites allocated for commercial building to be used to finance the redevelopment of less prosperous residential areas in the nearby 'twilight' zones.

Town planning is of enormous importance, and these proposals – more specific than the Conservatives' and more sensible than the Socialists' – provide the basis for intelligent action. Conservatives seem content to leave urban renewal to be carried out within the existing administrative and financial framework. This has not worked to date, and there is no reason to believe it will work in the future. Meanwhile the slums are spreading at least twice as fast as they have been cleared under the Tories.

5: New Homes for Old

Inadequate homes breed delinquency and apathy. So long as Britain is badly housed, people cannot be expected to overcome their grim resignation to life. Eighteen years after the war there are about $2\frac{1}{2}$ million people living in slums; more than 4 million people do not have a proper bath; 2 million people do not have an inside W.C.

Another $3\frac{1}{2}$ million householders are living in council houses, often in very dreary surroundings and hemmed in with restrictions. Too often the managers in municipal housing estates carry on like the benevolent squires: to argue that the rents are subsidized and that therefore tenants cannot be treated in the same way as owner-occupiers is to perpetuate meaningless class distinctions.

By contrast there are $6\frac{1}{2}$ million owner-occupiers who enjoy comparative freedom to make what improvements they see fit to their houses but suffer from the anarchy which surrounds home ownership in this country. Buying a house is unnecessarily complex, and it is still possible to buy a new house which might require as much as a third of a young executive's income by way of mortgage repayment, but which is sold without guarantee against defects of construction.

Almost all other dwellings, about $4\frac{1}{2}$ million, are occupied by tenants. These include the worst slums. A survey carried out by the Rowntree Trust in 1961–3 showed that over half of the households in privately rented properties in England and Wales had no fixed bath. 60,000 of these dwellings are being demolished each year by the local authorities as part of the slum-clearance programme. It will take till the end of the century at this rate to demolish all the slums occupied by private tenants which already exist, but by this time there will be another $2\frac{2}{3}$ million houses more than a hundred and twenty years old. There can be comparatively few houses built before 1880 which will count as satisfactory homes in the year 2000.

In spite of the fact that the worst slums are occupied by private tenants, the Conservative Government has done its utmost to discourage building to let. The 1959 Conservative Party Manifesto declared that 'local authorities will continue to play a big part in meeting housing needs'. But the fact is that local authorities have actually continued to play a steadily diminishing part. In 1953 the number of dwellings built by local authorities was 202,891, by 1963 this figure had fallen to 97,015.

Since private developers are building only some 2,000 dwellings for letting a year (mostly in the luxury class) and since many privately let houses are being pulled down every year as slums, the failure of the Conservative Government to allow local authorities to build for general needs is leading to a serious shortage of rented accommodation.

The result of this scarcity of houses and flats to let has been a general rise in rents in decontrolled property and racketeering in overcrowded houses. The Rachman affair spotlighted public attention on the way this shortage of rented accommodation had been used by some unscrupulous landlords for a sordid round of high rents, overcrowding, evictions, and re-letting at still higher rents. One hopes that the 1963 Housing Bill has strengthened the hands of local authorities to deal with these blots on the local landscape.

Rents and Rackets

The most alarming aspect of the Rachman affair remains, however, unsolved. Many of the local authorities, it was discovered, for one reason or another had chosen to turn a blind eye to the easy profiteering that had been going on in their boroughs. One reason for this unpardonable behaviour was that the boroughs were not willing to face up to the problem of the homeless they would have on their hands as a result of properties being condemned or upgraded. The situation is now arising again because the multi-occupied houses are being reduced in number as the landlords 'do them up' and re-let them for higher rents to a different class of customer.

In Britain in the 1960s families that can afford to pay £7 a week and more for two slum rooms are being turned out into the street. How does this situation arise? The first reason is quite simple. Britain has not been building enough houses, under either Labour or Conservative governments. In the fifteen years since the war England and Wales have only built 3,280,500 houses compared with 3,745,700 in the same period before the Second World War. In the peak year since the war, house-building in England and Wales, with much blowing of Conservative horns, touched 309,000 in 1954. This was easily surpassed in 1937 when house-building reached 347,000. Britain's rate of house-building is low compared with her European neighbours. In 1961–2 the U.K. rate of 6 houses built per 1,000 inhabitants was very low compared with the West German rate of 10·1, Sweden's 9·8, and Switzerland's 10·2 per 1,000 inhabitants. Only Belgium among the industrialized West European countries succeeded in building fewer houses than the U.K.

An obvious reason for the inadequacy of the British building effort is found in the backwardness of the building industry. It is characterized by small firms – there are 30,000 of them – and low wages. Productivity is low. Nothing like full advantage has been taken of new techniques and methods. Firms tender competitively for a single job and then take on and discharge labour on the same 'on–off' basis. If more continuity of work could be assured it would pay building firms to offer greater stability of employment and this in turn would justify more training schemes and higher wages and productivity.

The present government has not done nearly enough to encourage a higher rate of house-building in the private and public sector, and Liberals would set an immediate target of 375,000 per annum and a longer run target of 500,000 per annum. The failure of both Tories and Labour to reform the system of local government has meant that housing has been, with the exception of the L.C.C., the responsibility of the lowest tier of local government above the parish councils. The work of housing administration is performed by various local government departments including the clerk's department, the tradesmen's department, and the planning department. It is not a fluke that the L.C.C., the only county council which was a housing authority, replaced many of London's slums by architecturally famous blocks of flats.

Only when regional councils are set up will we be able to repeat throughout the country the advantages the L.C.C. brought to London housing. A regional authority can undertake not only the research and development necessary, but relate new ideas, materials, and 'new systems' to local authorities in their areas. Only regional authorities can afford to employ the best architects and specialized services and to hire these services to the local authorities. It is not surprising that the 1,400 local authorities, which on average build fewer than 34 houses each annually, cannot afford to take advantage of the prefabricated methods. As a result the average time of erection of a local-authority house in England and Wales is 12·4 months, and a block of flats 18·3 months. According to Mr Clive Barr, the Chief Architect at the Ministry of Housing, a number of systems of rationalized and industrialized construction are available, however, which have completed pilot groups of houses in under 3 months. This is another example of the opportunities Britain is missing by its failure to take advantage of a regional system of administration. At present prefabrication is used in only 5 per cent of all building in Britain, and mostly in schools and factories. Only about 24,000 system-houses a year are being built in Britain. However, in Scandinavia, where at least one house in ten is built by these methods, units consisting of bathroom, kitchen, and central-heating plant are delivered by lorry to the site. In France, for example, a building force less than two thirds the size of Britain's will put up 365,000 houses this year using mainly prefabricated methods. Meanwhile Britain's building industry lags behind. Productivity for all kinds of building work has crept up by only 2 per cent in 23 years.

National Building Code

Higher productivity would be best encouraged by the drawing up of a National Building Code designed to raise standards of construction, eliminate jerry-building, and encourage the use of up-to-date materials and techniques. At present the use of modern materials and procedures is prevented by out-dated by-laws. Another condition of progress is going to be greater flexibility on job demarcations. System-building will require greater flexibility on the part of the labour force as well as of management. Craft-training must provide in future that apprentices train not only for one currently established skill, but for groups of related skills between which the craftsman can move as the demand for his services changes. Any worker, skilled or unskilled, must also be able to re-qualify in a new grade when either his own career or the changing needs of the industry require it. Lastly, the Government must tackle restrictive practices in the building industry. The Monopolies Commission Report on the Building Industry revealed the existence of price rings, but no action has been taken by the President of the Board of Trade. Action to improve labour relations and work performance together with more competition in the supply and pricing of building material and fittings should provide a powerful incentive to lower costs and more efficient production in the industry.

The failure of the post-war Governments to build as many houses as pre-war has meant that slum clearance under the Labour and Conservative Governments has been completely inadequate. The Liberal party report on housing published in September 1962 recommended that the clearance rate must be trebled – from 60,000 to 180,000 slum dwellings cleared a year. This recommendation has since been borne out by a survey prepared by the Central Office of Information for the Ministry of Housing, the contents of which were revealed by the *Daily Herald* in July 1963. At first the government tried to keep the report a secret but after questions in the House it was placed in the Library of the House of Commons where the press revealed that it called for the replacement of two million houses within fifteen years followed by another three million in the following fifteen years. In short, slums are spreading twice as quickly as the Government can clear them.

This situation would never have arisen if the local authorities had not already had so many other building commitments. As the 1960 report of the Ministry admitted, many local authorities with numerous slum houses still to clear are faced with other extensive building commitments of various kinds. Consequently, they are usually working to the limit of their manpower resources – public health inspectors, architects, engineers and surveyors, legal staffs, building organization, and so on – and there is no easy way of supplementing these in a prosperous and fully employed economy.

If the local authorities have failed in the job of slum clearance the blame must mainly rest with the Ministry of Housing, which has thrust on these authorities the major task of providing municipal housing to the extent that their resources have been unable to cope with the broader functions of either effective planning or slum clearance.

There can be little doubt that housing policy got off on the wrong foot after the war because of the over-concentration of the Labour Government on council housing and an excessive zeal at the centre for detailed control from London. According to one commentator :

Ministerial approval was needed for every step of every housing project – for the selection of a site, the layout of the site, the plans of individual homes to be built on a site, advertisements for tenders and acceptances of a tender. . . . If the country already had enough good houses in the right places, and housing administration were confined to rent collection, repairs, and the management of transfers, then the local authorities could be left to get on with it, with the occasional guidance that they now get from the Minister and his Advisory Committee. Their present responsibilities for extensive new building, slum clearance redevelopment, and rehousing (including the rehousing of overspill population outside their borders) are clearly too much for them and could remain so even with administrative reform.*

Instead there must be placed at the service of the local authorities finance and specialist teams of architects, planners, and other building experts which would allow them to apply themselves more adequately to the task of slum clearance. A national survey of the condition and occupancy of existing dwellings must also be made. This survey must be based on uniform standards. The existing estimates of the extent of slum housing represented the number of dwellings the local authorities expected to clear rather than the actual needs. Hence the present slum clearance programme was based on figures which apparently showed that some London suburbs such as Carshalton had the same number of slums as St Pancras.

More should also be done to encourage people to participate in the running of their own housing estates. Council housing seems to be designed to undermine everything that should be encouraged. Their whole administration often seems designed to

* Stanley Alderston, *Housing* (Penguin Special, 1962).

emphasize that a tenant's housing depends not on his own choice and efforts but on the goodwill of the paternalistic local authority. The tenants are not consulted about the decor of their houses. There are often trivial regulations which cause great irritation and resentment. Lastly, council housing discourages movement. Once a council house is given up there is no guarantee that another can be secured in another locality.

Housing Associations

Housing associations on the other hand combine what is, in effect, a cost rent with a sense of personal responsibility for the houses and the neighbourhood. For some time now Liberals have been calling for steps to foster housing associations. The 1961 Housing Act had set up a capital fund of £25 million to be made available for loans to housing associations. The effects were very limited and only 4,000 houses a year were built as a result. This contrasts poorly with the situation in other European countries. In the Netherlands cooperative housing schemes account for nearly a quarter of all new housing, and in Sweden public housing schemes are usually organized on the lines of a 'daughter' co-operative, run by the tenants for each block of houses or flats, and a 'mother' cooperative supplying architectural, legal, and building services to a family of 'daughters'.

The 1962 Liberal housing report called for a really substantial scheme for the expansion of non-profit-making housing associations and recommended that the government should raise the funds available to at least £100 millions. The Government the following year brought in the 1963 Housing Bill which implemented this proposal. However, it is doubtful if housing cooperatives will really catch on in this country as long as the government pursues the kind of monetary policy it has favoured up to now and as long as the existing subsidy system is kept intact. Housing cooperatives in New York have been able to borrow money at 3 per cent and rebuild at 3¼ per cent. This has made it possible to reopen the centre of the city to lower–middle income families instead of barring it to all but the very rich and the poor, as increasingly happens in central London. In France the housing associations pay no interest in the first year and only 1 per cent in other years.

If interest rates were lower in Britain for non-profit-making housing associations it would be possible to slash the rents. At present the rents for new houses erected by these associations vary from £4 to £6 a week and can, in some areas, exceed £7. According to Mr Lionel Needleman in the National Institute's Economic Review for November 1961 only 23 per cent of families in Britain can afford to pay a rent of £4 (let alone £7) without spending more than a quarter of their pre-tax income on housing. One half of the rent of a new house is, however, accounted for by interest payment. A reduction in interest rates from just under 6 per cent to just under 4 per cent would be the equivalent to a slashing of building costs by 30 per cent.

This might require an element of subsidy in funds lent by the Government to the housing associations, although this would only arise if interest rates rose above 4 per cent.

Obviously one wants to avoid a situation where everyone is subsidizing everyone else's housing. On the other hand we must face up to the anomalies of the present situation whereby everyone in a council house receives a subsidy and owner-occupiers get substantial tax rebates on their mortgage interest payments, whereas the private tenants, and they are often the most deserving, get no subsidy from the State at all. Indeed, one of the biggest injustices in our society is our failure to relate housing subsidies to real needs. Young couples with small incomes and growing families are among the hardest hit. They have either to buy their houses at a time when they have many other commitments without being able to recoup a high proportion of their interest payments because they do not pay sufficient tax, or they pay free market rents – substantially higher than those of council tenants with the same incomes. Even council tenants who receive no rent rebate are generally paying much less for their housing than the less fortunate people who are not so high on the waiting list. One reason is that local authority rents are related to the original cost of the houses which is often very low because the houses were built when building costs were lower than today. In Leeds council rents were only 6d. a week until quite recently. Moreover local councils' financial calculations generally include heavy subsidies from the exchequer and the local rates. It is irrelevant today that a house may have cost only £300 to build in 1925. So long as people are willing to pay £4 a week rent for it today, any tenant who enjoys it for only 30s. a week is enjoying an advantage worth 50s. which is being denied to his fellow citizens.

Similarly a family buying a house and deducting the interest they pay on mortgage loans from their taxable income enjoy an advantage over a family which has to rent its own accommodation. According to Miss Nesbitt of the London School of Economics, this hidden subsidy means in effect that the rate of interest is reduced for those buying houses to 3·7 per cent at the standard rate of tax.

The introduction of subsidies through interest rates could easily be extended to housing associations and local authorities. The present housing subsidies are very complicated: each subsidy is calculated under a different Housing Act, and one level of subsidy is given for pre-war houses and another for post-war houses. If all these subsidies were swept away a subsidy could be paid fixed at the standard rate of tax paid on every £ paid. Miss Nesbitt has calculated that in the case of the metropolitan borough of Camberwell the proposed new subsidy tied to the standard rate of tax would have amounted to £321,625 compared with £316,871 already received. This example is particularly interesting as it shows that if tax relief granted by the Government at present to owner-occupiers was extended to Camberwell it would work out slightly higher than the existing exchequer subsidy. The same tax relief could be extended to housing associations regardless of whether the tenants have an equity interest in the association or not. At present the 1963 Housing Bill restricts tax relief to tenants who have a share in the capital.

These proposals would meet the needs of families moving into new rented property. Professor Donnison has drawn attention to the importance of providing housing to let to accommodate people who want to move. A survey of private householders in England made in March 1962 found that 33 per cent of the 14 million householders in England either wanted to move or believed they were likely to move in the following year. Half of those wanting to move had taken some deliberate step to move house; and two thirds of them wanted to rent, and a third to buy. Those who fail to buy when young may never get another chance, for a large proportion of our population still attains its maximum earning power before the age of 20. As these people reach their forties their opportunities of borrowing money disappear. This point has been emphasized by the Liberal party. The 1962 Liberal housing report called for special 'housing pools' to encourage movement.

Certainly many people will continue to be frustrated and the economy will suffer as long as housing to let remains in short supply. The N.E.D.C. report *Conditions Favourable To Faster Growth* suggested a special housing subsidy in excess of the general one to provide an incentive for local councils to build houses for transferred workers. This might be done as a stop-gap. Council houses are usually given to manual workers, however, and it is essential that the movement of skilled men should also be encouraged. If either housing associations could borrow their capital more cheaply or all housing associations got tax relief, a major step would have been taken in the right direction.

Housing Jungle

Another major obstacle to the free movement of families is the near anarchy which surrounds buying and selling a house. House-buying is an unnecessary jungle. It remains complex for lack of a straightforward system of registering and transferring land ownership and changes. Compulsory registration of title to land throughout Britain would reduce the amount of work which solicitors claim is required in investigating a title, and the Law Society would thus be made to look again at the scale of fees involved in house purchase. (But even under the present system a House Owners' Society, recently founded in Harrow, Middlesex, has been reported as charging about one third of the average solicitor's fees for selling a house and less than half for buying on a mortgage.)

Cooperative movements should be encouraged among owners as well as tenants. The service of an owners' cooperative could be invaluable both to the owners as individuals and to their neighbours. In building and buying a house, in its maintenance, insurance, and taxation, in schemes of exterior decoration and common amenities, an owners' association could play a valuable role. Also local authorities should be all able to grant 100 per cent loans to house purchasers. And it was a Liberal Council, in Orpington, which first agreed to take into account the earnings of the wife in the computation of the amount of a house loan.

Since the Orpington by-election the Government has gone some way to meet Liberal demands for the abolition of Schedule A tax, which had become a tax on ignorance. The Liberal Party now wants the remaining tax obstacles to owner-occupation removed. Profits tax should be removed on building societies. This would cost the Exchequer only £4 million a year, but it has been estimated that the removal of profits tax would enable interest rates on mortgages to be cut by ¼ per cent, which would save £100 of interest charges on a twenty-year loan of £2,500. The case for levying profits tax on building societies is hard to justify. It would be more logical to abolish profits tax and income tax on their surpluses and their replacement by a tax on any surplus where the reserve fund exceeds a specified proportion of total assets. This could encourage the more progressive building societies to charge lower interest rates.

There is also no reason why longer-period mortgage loans should not be made available to people in lower-income groups. The Government could undertake to ensure mortgages for periods of up to thirty-five years where the people concerned are 'sound risks' but unable to repay the loans out of income over shorter periods and also where the properties are either new or recently constructed. A scheme of this kind could also be used to encourage the granting of mortgages on flats as well as houses by building societies and local authorities. This is uncommon in England and Wales but is frequently done in Scotland. Not only would this foster home ownership; it would also encourage private enterprise to build more flats for sale.

If the Government shows imagination and allows the local authorities to take advantage of a regional pool of expertise, and if vested interests are not allowed to prevent progress, the housing problem can be solved. But it will take Liberal plans to do it.

6: Reshaping Transport

In all sorts of ways transport in this country is in a mess. British Railways lost £136 million last year, largely because much of its capacity is under-utilized; the British Road Federation estimates that traffic congestion cost the nation another £500 million because road space was over-used; meanwhile in the cities, during the rush hour, public transport is grossly overcrowded, whereas in the countryside buses and trains are being withdrawn because there is insufficient demand for their services.

Moreover the situation is deteriorating rapidly, and the remedies proposed by the Government to date are only stop-gaps. Dr Beeching's axe is a blunt instrument. The closure of the railway lines, even on a massive scale, cannot by itself provide Britain with a transport system of the right shape. It could, if pursued independently of other transport developments, lead to a further clogging of the road arteries of the country which are already costing the nation more than the railway deficit.

Railways and Beeching
It must be remembered that the railways were still making a small profit when the Tories came to power. Since then the position has got rapidly out of control. In spite of the very large capital investment of £1,240 million which has been made in the railways since 1951, the Beeching Report has shown that more than half the stations do not make enough money to pay for the cost of the stations themselves, and one third of the route mileage carries only 1 per cent of the freight.

We now know that the massive investment made in the railways in the fifties was mainly wasted. The 1955 Modernization Plan was hastily approved by the Government as a result of the alarm in government circles at mounting losses. After nearly two decades of disinvestment in the railways, for which the Labour Government must carry part of the blame, investment was stepped up suddenly. As, before 1959, British Railways calculated the reduction in a prospective loss as a profit, it is not surprising that the Modernization Plan was condemned by a

Select Committee of the House of Commons as being 'merely a hotch-potch of the things that the Commission was saying it was desirable to achieve by 1970, ill qualified, and not readily explainable'. The Ministry of Transport never inquired into the details of the Plan. In any case it did not have any economists who were qualified to examine it. In 1959, according to the Select Committee Report, 'it became doubtful whether the Plan would bring in the profits that had been hoped for . . . and the Ministry began to ask for a much more detailed justification of the schemes on which the money was to be spent. . . Thus for the first time the Ministry became aware of the way in which the Commission's figures had been calculated. What they learnt came as a shock.'

Is the nation going to get another shock when the Beeching Report is examined in five years' time? Certainly it is based on a much clearer picture of why the railway losses are being incurred. Its claims are also more conservative than the original Modernization Plan. This time the investment thought to be necessary is £250 million, compared with the £1,660 million asked for in the revised Plan and the £1,100 million already spent. In theory it seems obvious that passenger and freight travel by rail should be more profitable when concentrated on the dense traffic flows between major centres of population and industry. But there is no evidence that the Beeching Report (any more than the Modernization Plans) considered the alternative transport investments which are open. As pointed out in the Hall Report *Transport Needs over the Next Twenty Years* (which was published by the Ministry of Transport almost at the same time as Beeching but seems to have been prepared completely independently) demand for transport in practice depends on the location of industry which is itself influenced by the availability of transport. Transport policy, in other words, cannot be considered in isolation from the other problems involved in regional planning. Yet the Government asked Dr Beeching to put forward proposals for reshaping the railway system without undertaking any assessment of the alternative road investments or the needs arising from future patterns of regional development.

Buchanan

The Buchanan Report has shown that any organized attempt to solve the problem of traffic in towns must involve the large-scale redevelopment of our cities and towns. This will also require a regional approach. The study group under Sir Geoffrey Crowther, which acted as a steering group for the Buchanan Report, is emphatic that the existing system of local authority planning cannot cope and suggests the formation of Regional Development Agencies. But the Crowther proposals for Regional Development Agencies do not go far enough: it is proposed to form these regional agencies only for 'each recognizable urban region' and not necessarily to cover the whole country. If certain regions which are already in great need of rejuvenation are not to be left out of the advantages of regional administration it will be necessary to get the administrative framework right from the beginning. Furthermore it is not obvious from the Crowther proposals whether there would be any democratic control of the proposed agencies. Apart from this major proviso Liberals would agree wholeheartedly with the Crowther Report's findings that transport in the towns – we would add in the countryside – will not be satisfactorily tackled without a regional framework of government. At present town planning is in the hands of over 100 planning authorities, which includes the county councils and the large urban authorities. The Ministry of Housing and Local Government is supposed to coordinate the local plans but it clearly will be unable to do so as long as it has detailed commitments in the field of housing and as long as there is no clear statement of national planning objectives. Only when a high-level unit – a Ministry of Regional Development – has drawn up a national strategy on the overall distribution of industry and population will it be possible to coordinate local development plans.

The Conservative Government has argued that the town and not the region 'must make its own Buchanan decision'. These were Sir Keith Joseph's words in the debate on the Buchanan Report in the House of Commons on 10 February 1964. He went on: 'When it comes to make that decision we all know that road and parking policy within an urban community acts and reacts on all the other elements of the town. It acts and reacts on housing, schools, colleges, universities, recreation, and places of work. Above all, it acts and reacts on the character of the town itself. These surely must be local issues.'

This statement by the Minister of Housing is tantamount to a rejection of the Buchanan Report. It is pointless to accept its proposals and then refuse to implement the machinery necessary to apply these remedies. It is not enough to argue that each town must strike a balance between traffic and environment. Of course they must. But the balance can only be established as part of a regional development. As already pointed out, the local authorities have been unable to tackle the job of slum clearance because they do not have enough qualified people to do the job. Nor do they have the financial resources. Even if they were given more finance by the Government, there would still remain the overriding objection that transport development can be shaped only within the terms of reference of the region it will serve.

Investment Policy and Regional Planning

The Tories have condemned the country to another decade of frustration by their failure to reform the system of local government. Now they argue that Buchanan is a long-term affair and must await the reorganization of local government. But the strangulation of our cities will not wait. Even if it could, there is no sign that the reshuffling of local boundaries as recommended by the Royal Commission would give us the positive framework we require. If they cannot cope with Rutland how can they throw up a solution for Britain in the motor age? What we need is positive transport planning for the future. At present both central government and local authority planning are at least inadequate and at worst non-existent. Trunk roads and motorways are the responsibility of the Ministry of Transport, but the Board of Trade controls the siting of industrial though not commercial buildings. Each of these authorities has its own priorities and resources – not to mention that through Dr Beeching British Railways, in the absence of any effective national strategy on the part of the Government towards transport, is seeking to concentrate all the new freight centres in the existing big towns. No consideration has been taken of the increased traffic on the already congested roads. No new freight depots are being sited in relation to growth points. On the contrary only a few freight depots are to be situated outside the already crowded coffin of the Manchester–London axis. There will be only four new freight depots in the north-east, three in South Wales, and two in the West Country. The new liner trains will run on routes paralleled almost exactly by the planned motorways and improved roads.

The result of this uncoordinated development is obvious. It is a formula for national thrombosis. If we go on as we are (and it is estimated that there will be forty million vehicles on the roads by the end of the century), either there will have to be extensive restrictions on the use of cars or we shall all be condemned to continuous frustration and the eventual seizing up of communications.

What is the alternative? The key to transport problems is a coordinated investment policy at the centre and positive regional planning in the provinces implementing the national transport strategy. The Ministry of Transport must be responsible for drawing up comparisons of the returns which could be expected from major investments in the different transport sectors. Up till now the major decisions – for example the railway electrification programme for the London–Crewe line – have been approved on the basis of the most rudimentary criteria without regard for alternatives such as the M1 motorway. The Ministry of Transport must consider first the overall level of investment, secondly how this must be divided between road and rail, and thirdly how the road investment should be divided between urban and inter-urban roads. These investment decisions must not be considered in isolation but in relation to other aspects of town and country planning. This should be the task of the high-level unit coordinating national strategy in the area of town and country planning and regional development. For instance, the M1 analysis showed a reasonably high rate of return on the new motorway. But the calculations did not consider the costs of congestion, delays, and long journeys to work at either end of the M1; yet these costs are almost certainly bound to rise as the M1 reinforces the attraction of London and Birmingham. More experts are required in a Ministry of Transport to assess the social as well as the economic benefit of transport investment. The Road Research Laboratory has pioneered studies of the traffic flow and time savings resulting from the construction of the M1. These must now be used by the Ministry in comparing all new investments and their secondary effects. Recently the Victoria Line (in London Transport's underground system) which previously had failed to get the consent of the Ministry of Transport on commercial grounds was found to be profitable as a result of the indirect benefits which will accrue to the community. The greatest single benefit will be savings on the surface to road users as a result of faster traffic flows. There is no evidence that skilled assessments of this kind have been used by Conservative Transport Ministers in comparing alternative road investment schemes. (By contrast, Dr Beesley, who was joint author of both the M1 and the Victoria Line studies, is an active Liberal.) These techniques can be applied to small schemes as well as large ones and must be used to assess the comparative values of all major road and rail development.

They will not yield automatic answers, but these techniques would put judgement on transport policy on a surer basis and avoid the catastrophic errors of the past.

If, at the same time, the transport users pay for the cost of every individual journey (in so far as they can be calculated) or when there is a subsidy this is made explicit, it will be possible to allocate transport resources in a much more efficient manner than has hitherto been the case. The Labour party seems to think that transport should be provided as an integrated public service. Public transport, Socialists say, should be available everywhere, to everyone who needs it, as a right. Furthermore, they argue that to ensure that everyone plays fair it is necessary to integrate everyone into the same organizations, subject to central directives. Only then, it is argued, will every transport job – profitable or not – be undertaken by means of the transport best suited to do it.

The Labour answer is superficially attractive, although, as the Beeching Report has underlined, the cost of keeping unremunerative lines open, by financing services which do not pay through cross-subsidization, would be very expensive to the rest of the community. Another fundamental criticism is that the Labour policy – as always – does not indicate the criteria by which they would take planning decisions. To economic and technical problems they pose administrative solutions.

Administrative integration in the post-war Labour Government, however, did not achieve effective coordination of investment under the 1947 transport system. In the words of an excellent article in the April 1963 issue of *Socialist Commentary*: 'Suppose road goods haulage, "C" licences, railways, taxicabs, aeroplanes, road planning, even the motor industry were all made into departments of a monster Department of Transport Planning, what would the department do? How would it start a plan? What criteria would it bring to bear upon these problems?'

The other socialist dogma, that transport must be operated as a public service, is equally fallacious. There are certain classes of people who may depend completely upon public transport, for example some country dwellers. They have a strong case for subsidized transport. But travellers in general are not particularly poor people any more than people who buy books or clothes. On what grounds should they be subsidized? If a Labour government gives general subsidies to transport there will inevitably be less for education, hospitals, and slum clearance.

The only general class of people whom Liberals would be prepared to consider subsidizing are the commuters. The Buchanan Report has shown that road traffic will double and redouble in the next two decades. Buchanan considers that sane and civilized living in cities requires 'good cheap public transport'. Dr Beeching, on the other hand, argues that railways should concentrate on their most profitable business, which is fast inter-city passenger services and fast long-distance freight trains. In the Beeching system of thinking some surburban and commuter services, even in the London area, ought to go. Liberals consider that social-benefit analysis would show that in some cases the subsidizing of commuter services would pay by relieving congestion on the roads and preventing ribbon development along roads. But the repercussions to the country as a whole of subsidizing commuters' travel in, say, the London region would first be examined, for this might only accelerate the drift to the south.

The Liberal party, however, unlike the Labour party, believe that the most efficient transport system is the one based on the demand of the transport users. Apart from special cases, for instance, some country dwellers and some commuters, people should have freedom of choice in the use of transport services so long as they are willing to pay for what they use. Only the person concerned can know which of the alternative means available is the most convenient. There are always a large number of considerations relevant – the cost of the journey, the time taken, how fragile the goods are, and so on. No nationalized transport concern – no matter how many sub-offices it has – can make the choice as efficiently as the individual concerned.

Charges

If the transport system is to represent the most efficient use of resources it is necessary that prices reflect costs and that taxation does not distort the consumer choice. The current pricing system as it effects the choice of the commuter between public and private transport is distorted by the fact that road users do not pay their full costs and secondly by the railways' providing and maintaining their own track. The new parking charges are a step towards making the private motorist pay for the congestion he creates. The level of parking charges should vary from one big city to another and take into account the time of day in order to take account of congestion created. However, there is an obvious limit to the price of parking: it cannot be raised to a point where only the very rich can afford to park in the West End. The Liberal party report on transport also recommended in September 1962 that consideration should be given to the use of meters on cars which could be made to be activated on entry of the vehicle to a congested zone. The motorist would receive a bill at, say, quarterly intervals for the charges incurred.

One essential complement to such a pricing policy, however, must be the provision of adequate roads for the by-passing of congested areas. Major routes round or through cities need to be designed with limited access in order to provide for a faster flow of traffic. Clearly there will have to be a congestion tax in order that the private motorist is forced to face up to the social costs he creates by using road space in congested areas. At present the commuter tends to compare the daily fare charged by public transport with the cost of petrol consumed on the journey. The result is that more and more commuters are switching from public transport to private cars which take up far more road space. But the congestion tax need not be another tax on top of the existing charges borne by British motorists. All that is required is the replacement of the existing vehicle and licence duties by a tax on the use of congested road space. It has been estimated that it costs £150 a year to keep a car in the London area. This means that something like £225 million a year are spent on standing charges which are hardly taken into account when assessing the daily cost of commuter travel. London Transport and British Railways, however, have to recoup as far as possible their overheads and operating costs through fares. Altogether these amount to £130 million. If part of the motorists' standing charges are translated into a running cost the pricing mechanism will begin to operate in favour of public transport.

A new lease of life could also be given to Britain's public transport through greater use of differential rates between rush-hour and off-peak travel. Commuter fares are high because the uneven flow of commuter travel necessitates the provision of equipment which is under-utilized for most of the day. Any reduction of fares which would encourage people to travel at off-peak hours would help to spread the load. On the London underground and British Railways in the London Region and elsewhere there are already special shopping returns. But the extent of these practices is nothing like sufficient. Differential charges, especially on a season ticket for travel the hour before and the hour after the rush hour, combined with much more strenuous efforts to obtain the staggering of working hours, could provide us with weapons with which to tackle the problems of congestion.

Relating the taxation of motor vehicles to the congestion they cause and abolishing motor vehicle and licence duties would help the people who live in the countryside. But this is not the whole answer to the problem of rural transport. The Jack Committee on rural bus services pointed out in its report (1961) that though the growth of rural car ownership diminished 'the number of persons who experienced hardship or inconvenience, the degree of hardship or inconvenience which they experience may tend to increase as services are reduced'. In particular, where railway services are withdrawn a subsidy will be required for the local bus services. This should be done on a regional basis. The Government is seeking to minimize the effect of the railway closures by emphasizing that bus services will be reorganized to link up with railheads, and Mr Marples has been reported as saying that in most cases even in remote parts of the country the buses will run without subsidy by cross-subsidizing lean routes from profitable ones. This is complex eye-wash. The bus services have been losing passengers more rapidly than the railways in the last decade. The result is that the urban routes which previously subsidized the unprofitable country services are themselves running at a loss. It is true that the Railway Board frequently subsidize substitute bus services when they withdraw a service. But if this is continued after the Beeching Report is implemented even in part, there will be little hope of reducing the size of the British Railways deficit. In any case the existing subsidies are not determined according to any clear social criteria but as a result of local pressure.

The regional authorities will be able to consider the question of subsidizing transport in the context of regional development. For transport is not only a means of getting from one place to another; it is an instrument of inducing people to move and settle in another place. New transport lines can bring a new impetus to a declining region and create new opportunities. So far this key role of new transport links seems to have escaped the Government. Not only have they shown no enthusiasm for building motorways as a means of opening up declining regions, but they have also overlooked the positive role the motorways can play in attracting development to regions between the existing conurbations. A classic case is provided by the projected route of the M4. The Ministry of Transport first proposed one route which was withdrawn after bitter opposition had been provoked in defence of the Berkshire Downs. The second proposed route, like the first, took into account only that the motorway should be as direct as possible and should pass near the only two large centres, Reading and Swindon. The fact that their line passed through an area where the development of another town of this size will be very difficult did not seem to concern the Ministry of Transport. However the Minister of Housing is known to be concerned about the need to encourage new towns as large as Swindon and Reading to accommodate the needs of the London region before the year 1980.

Regional plans are also required to provide the only criteria by which rail closures can finally be judged. British Railways are considering the closures of many stations in areas which are scheduled as development districts. There are also many lines threatened which could be required in the future to link the new towns which will be developing round existing centres. This is not an argument for keeping every line open indiscriminately. It is a strong reason for scrapping the existing system of Transport Users Consultative Committees and handing over to regional authorities the power to keep a line open through paying the Railways Board a subsidy or else providing for alternative means of public transport when there are either developments or social grounds for so doing. The existing inquiries are a farce. The 1962 Transport Act gives them no statutory authority for inquiring into freight service closures, and they may not question proposals to reduce the number of passenger trains. Only the complete cessation of passenger services now falls within their terms of reference, and even then they can only advise the Minister on the degree of hardship involved. Moreover the Act lays down that each decision must be taken by the Committee as a whole. Although small groups of members can make particular cases their responsibility, there is no machinery at present for integrating the machinery for considering subsidies in the context of any regional development plans.

Safety

It is not enough, however, to ensure that Britain is able to take advantage of the motor age without dislocating our cities and the countryside. We must also prevent an increase in the number of cars on the roads leading to a mounting death toll. According to the findings of a two and half years' investigation undertaken for the Road Research Laboratory, one in five motorists questioned after being seriously injured in road crashes admitted that they had been drinking shortly before their accidents. Dr

Collister, who relied on questions and made no test other than smelling the breath, was reported in the *Observer* as saying that tests made by other doctors in hospitals in Manchester and Derby disclosed that 47 to 48 per cent of road casualties had taken alcohol. The Liberal Transport Report recommended that it should be made an offence to drive a vehicle when there is 0.05 per cent or more of alcohol in the blood. This is roughly equivalent to having drunk three whiskies or 1½ pints of beer on an empty stomach. Liberals believe that Britain is now ready for legislation on this question. Mr Marples has gone on record as saying that he believes the problem is really a matter for the Church.

7: Investment in People

Britain is unable to come to terms with the 1960s because her education is out of date and insufficient for the needs of the nation. Under the Tories the educational system is geared to the needs of an élite. It is no excuse that they were waiting for Robbins. The people for whom the crash programme is now being devised were born in the immediate post-war years. The Crowther Report pointed out in 1959 the increase in university places needed to meet the growth in sixth forms. The fundamental reason why the Conservatives have failed to provide the educational opportunities the country requires is their static view of society; they have failed or been unwilling to grasp the significance of education as an agent of change.

For education is an instrument of growth: not just economic growth (although this does depend on the breadth of educational opportunity) but the growth of individual freedom and happiness which ultimately hinges on the quality of our educational system. Educational advance depends upon freedom and experiment, though Socialist policy does not acknowledge this. It is the task of the educational system to give everyone, as far as possible, the amount and kind of education he wants. This in turn depends on the ability of the educational authorities to adapt and change their teaching to meet the changing needs of society. The State cannot assist the growth of every individual by his own effort and to the full potentiality of his own personality by imposing an educational system which is based, with whatever good intentions, on what the Government thinks would be good for the people.

At a time when there is a substantial degree of agreement within the country that education must be given a higher priority, it is all the more important that the basis of any massive investment programme is right. Liberals have been calling for a doubling of expenditure on education since the 1961 Liberal Assembly. After the Orpington by-election the Tories published a leaflet condemning Liberals as 'glib' and 'irresponsible' for advocating a doubling of Government expenditure on education and our road system. Now they have changed their tune and are willing to endorse almost any target and incorporate it in their modernization programme. But people are not easily persuaded by a government which one year rejects the estimates made by the University Grants Committee of the grants needed for university expansion to reach a target of 170,000 places by 1972–3 and the following year (the day after the publication of a Royal Commission Report) publishes a White Paper accepting the recommendation of 197,000 university places by 1967–8.

Development Programme

A ten-year development programme for education is a necessity. This forward plan for education should have as its objective the development of every child's capabilities. It should not be a detailed, immutable blueprint. But if the objectives are to be attained there must be a programme with dates fixed in the future for the execution of its component parts. Admirable as the work of the Ministry of Education has been in many ways, it cannot in recent years be said to have shown effective or far-sighted leadership. As usual, an important reason for the lack of overall planning has been the preoccupation of Ministries and top officials with details of policy which could be better left to others.

In some fields, the result of the concentration of the Ministry with details has been that planning has been controlled by the local authorities. This is true of the structure and the pattern of the school system. In other fields – in both the curriculum and the method of teaching – there has been little coordination; with the result that what is taught in schools is largely controlled at different stages by the G.C.E. and the eleven-plus examination. Unfortunately neither the Minister nor the local authorities have had at their disposal any adequate research facilities by which they could test some of the assumptions on which the present system is based. Instead the education system has gone on living under certain questionable hypotheses, many of which seem to radicals to contain the symptoms of our maladjustment to modern requirements. One example is premature and excessive specialization; another is the concept of streaming in primary schools; a third the failure of English education to concern itself with teaching technical subjects to bright boys and girls.

Clearly any programme of educational advance will have to challenge these assumptions. There will have to be more overall planning and research into many aspects of education. If there is to be more planning and control the big question remains: over what and by whom should the control be exercised? The essential difference between Labour and Liberal policies in education is that Labour has chosen to ignore this question because socialists prefer authority to freedom. The Liberal party has given considerable thought to this question and considers that a regional system of educational administration would create the balance of power within the system required to permit a programme of educational advance without fear that the result would be either an increase in the power of the State or a perpetuation of the regional disparities which already exist in Britain.

Regional Planning

The regional councils would plan and provide surveys for the whole region but leave day-to-day administration in the hands of the boroughs. A regional system would do much to remedy inequalities of opportunity arising from the differences which at present exist between large and small authorities, at present ranging from Birmingham with its population of more than a million down to Canterbury with its 30,500. Secondly it would diminish the problems which arise from the existence of rich and poor local authorities; 74 out of the 82 local education authorities whose pupil-teacher ratio will exceed the national average in 1963 are in the north; 73 per cent of the local authorities who have less than 14 out of every 100 13-year-olds in their grammar schools are also in the north. Thirdly it would diminish the difficulties which arise from the local authority boundaries. Under a regional system it would be easier for children to cross local education boundaries to go to school. Lastly, and perhaps most important of all, it would make possible the establishment of regional authorities who could finance research projects into new techniques and fresh approaches to our educational problems.

If there had not been one regional authority in England, the L.C.C., it is more than likely that comprehensive schools would have been much slower to achieve recognition in the rest of the country. On the other hand if a Labour Government had been in power throughout the 1950s the chances are that the Government would have launched a massive building programme on the local authorities based on the large comprehensive schools favoured by the L.C.C. However, as the Fabian Socialists are beginning to realize, there are considerable advantages in other forms of non-selective secondary education. Liberals, and in particular Mr A. D. C. Peterson, the Liberal Party spokesman on education, have been advocating for some years the virtues of the Leicestershire plan, in which children go to common high schools from 11 to 14 and can then choose to go on to 'upper schools' if they agree to stay till they are 16. The advantages of this plan are not only that the pressure of examinations on the primary and high schools has eased but that the variety of courses offered to older children is wider and the G.C.E. results are slightly better in the areas of the plan than they are in the selective grammar schools in Leicestershire. Furthermore it is not necessary to embark on a programme which would involve rebuilding all our secondary schools because under the Leicestershire plan the existing buildings can be used as either common high schools or upper schools.

A phased programme of educational advance must therefore be launched in the knowledge that the power of the State will be balanced by new regional education authorities. The first priority of both the national and the regional plan must be a massive expansion of higher education to reduce the teacher shortage. The Liberal party had called for a doubling of the present full-time places in higher education in the next ten years some months before the Robbins Report was published. Robbins showed that the Liberal target of 400,000 places in higher education by 1973 was borne out by detailed analysis which calculated that 392,000 places were required 1973–4. It is, however, questionable whether the Robbins Report goes far enough in its longer-term objectives. Robbins wants to raise the 8 per cent at present enjoying full-time higher education of the relevant age group to 17 per cent by 1980. Mr Grimond, in particular, has criticized this as inadequate; 'It may, of course, be totally impracticable to take in everybody who wants to go to university, but suppose it were practicable, should we want to do so? In my opinion we should want to do so, and in my opinion even today we should aim at giving as many people as possible the opportunity of at least spending a year or two at university.'

Beyond Robbins

We must go beyond Robbins if we are going to create an open society out of the existing social pattern. The goal must be to make enough places in higher education for a place to be available for every boy and girl wanting to go on to a degree. America has an open system and the result is that half of young Americans now go on to college; it is estimated that by 1980 two thirds may reasonably be expected to do so.

Robbins, it is true, has made one hole in the Tory bulwarks. Once and for all the report has exploded the concept of a static pool of ability. Prior to the report Conservatives had argued that there was only a small percentage of the population – around 4 per cent – who could benefit from a university education. Mr Henry Brooke, then Chief Secretary to the Treasury, in a debate in the House of Commons on 5 April 1962 equated a larger proportion of people entering university with a corresponding increase in 'failed B.A.s'. In the same debate Sir Edward Boyle said 'if the universities can match with student places this [birth-rate] rise of 35 per cent over five years, then we shall be entitled to say that no one has had a reduced chance of getting to a university through being born in the top year of the bulge. That would be an achievement of which the nation could be proud'. In other words the Tories (at least till their dramatic *volte-face* after the publication of the Robbins Report) thought it would be a considerable achievement to provide 4 per cent of an expanding population with university places.

The Robbins Report has demonstrated beyond reasonable doubt that the flow of talent from secondary schools remains blocked by unequal opportunities. For the Government has not even been capable of maintaining the proportion of the relevant age groups entering university. In 1959 6.1 per cent of the age group gained the minimum entrance qualifications and 4.2 per cent got places; three years later the comparable figures were 7 per cent and 4 per cent. The growth of sixth forms has been going on at the rate of 5 per cent per annum. In eight years there has been a 72 per cent increase in the number of school-leavers with five or more O-level passes, and of more than 100 per cent in the output of students with two or more A-level passes.

In view of this doubling of the number of students leaving school with two or more A-level passes in the last eight years the Robbins projections must be considered conservative. There is nothing ambitious about a target of 10 per cent of the relevant age group in universities and C.A.T.s by 1980. In fact Robbins takes no account of raising the school-leaving age to 16 and assumes that the existing entrance standards will be maintained, although these requirements are much higher than in many other countries.

It is true that the Robbins Report accepts the general principle of the need for an open system of higher education – 'that courses of higher education should be available for all those who are qualified by ability and attainment to pursue them and who wish to do so' – but its insistence on maintaining the existing entrance standards robs the acceptance of the principle of its value.

Admission standards in Britain are higher than in most European universities, and are higher than before the war, because they are a form of rationing made necessary by the scarcity of places. A slight relaxation of these standards – in 1961–2 83 per cent of university entrants had at least three A-level passes – would not involve a dilution of academic standards. If the level of attainment of students at present entering universities is not all that it might be (Kingsley Amis has complained that is impossible to teach English at university level to students who have not even been taught what metre is at school) it is precisely because teaching standards in schools have fallen on account of the growing proportion of teachers who are non-graduate. A relaxation of standards would diminish the risk of producing a meritocracy. It would also interrupt the vicious tendency towards premature specialization in schools and produce pupils better able to take advantage of higher education. It is true that Robbins has attacked some of the elements associated with an élite university system. The C.A.T.s are to be included, and some colleges of education. A resolution passed by the Liberal Party Council in February 1963 called for a closer integration of

teacher-training colleges with other forms of higher education
and the development of C.A.T.s into technological universities.

Robbins extends the frontiers of higher education to all work
beyond Higher National Certificate and G.C.E. A-level, pro-
posing a flexible pattern of institutions which will allow students
to move from one college to another in place of the hierarchy
of non-university institutions we have at present, with its distinctions, segregation, and diversity of treatment by different
authorities. This is fine, but it stops short of opening up the
university system to incorporate all institutions of higher
education.

Instead we want to see a wide-open-door policy for British
universities. This does not mean lowering the existing standards
of the existing universities, but it does require the setting up of
new liberal arts colleges on the American model. These would
supply liberal arts and science courses of a non-functional and
non-technical nature. Some of these liberal arts colleges would
become undergraduate colleges of new universities. This is a role
that could be performed by some of the most distinguished
public schools, whose staff are well capable of teaching at university level and whose scholars are already working at the level of
some of the distinguished American liberal arts colleges. Thus
Winchester and Eton might become undergraduate departments.
The graduate schools might be New College, Oxford, or King's
College, Cambridge, which respectively are on the same foundation, or else they might be attached to or be the centre of a new
university in Windsor and Winchester. Only when the universities are 'wide open' will it be possible to claim that higher
education for all has arrived.

In fact, of course, Oxford and Cambridge colleges have been
varying their entrance standards for years in order to allow an
intake of a good 'cross-section' of undergraduates. According to
Ziman and Rose,* 'Year by year, the examiners deliberately set
questions which will not expose the weakness of candidates. Year
by year they allow semi-literate and totally ignorant undergraduates to slide into an honours degree.'

Robbins raised doubts about whether the present methods of

* *Camford Observed* (Gollancz, 1964).

selection at Oxford and Cambridge have results that are socially just. In 1961–2 some 39 per cent of all undergraduates at Oxford and 25 per cent at Cambridge were from schools maintained by local education authorities. At the remaining universities in England and Wales the proportion was 70 per cent. But, as Brian Jackson has pointed out, the Oxbridge students are more than a social élite;* they are an academic élite too: 39 per cent of the men have at least three A-levels with marks of more than 60 per cent. This is double the proportion found in other universities. It is also probably one of the reasons why the colleges are willing to 'drop' their entrance qualifications for a man or woman who has abilities in a different direction. This is probably a good thing or else Oxbridge would develop into a tighter intellectual élite than it is at present. On the other hand it is undesirable if the good 'all-rounders' come from only the private or the direct grant schools. One way to break the 'stranglehold' of Oxbridge for the cleverest school-leavers would be to develop more post-graduate schools in place of any further expansion of undergraduate places. Some dons are good at research and appalling at lecturing, while others are best at teaching. If there were more post-graduate schools one might find that the former would fit in better teaching graduate students in seminars while the latter would be able to spend more time than they do at present actually teaching. Robbins has hinted that there is need for further investigation of Oxford and Cambridge. Radicals would endorse this viewpoint; 'fairie lands' in the middle of Britain must be reconciled with a dynamic society.

The role of the university must change in a changing society. The courses in institutions of higher education must be modernized, and in particular less specialized degree courses with a greater relevance to the intellectual basis of contemporary problems and economic life must be created. There is also much to be said for undergraduates taking a general degree first, or at least spending a first year on general studies before embarking on a specialist course. The curse of amateurism must be tackled at the roots, in the schools and universities themselves. The scientist and the non-scientist have been hampered for too long by excessive specialization which prevents each from understanding the

* 'The Oxbridge Stranglehold', *Where* (January 1964).

other's point of view. These general courses could be taught with more than seven students per teacher (the average ratio which is endorsed by Robbins). Modern techniques, closed-circuit television, and teaching machines for languages would permit larger classes on the general courses. It would then be possible to decide more accurately which students could benefit from specialization.

Teachers

The crux of educational advance, however, will remain the quality and quantity of teachers and teaching. We need at least 100,000 teachers in training by 1973. Over the next few years we shall have an increasingly desperate teacher shortage; 60,000 more teachers in addition to the 300,000 in service are needed today to stop classes being oversized. During the next decade the school population is expected to increase by almost a million, from 6.9 million in 1960 to 7.8 million in 1970. To allow for this increase and to bring down class sizes to their regulation number, an extra 100,000 teachers will have to be recruited. The Tories have more or less admitted that they have failed to solve this problem. Sir Edward Boyle said in February 1963: 'I do not want to hold out any hopes that this [their enlarged training programme of 80,000 places for teacher training by 1970] will lead to an early reduction in the size of classes. All our efforts will be needed to hold classes to their present level during the next decade.'

It is not surprising that the Tories do not expect to be able to attract sufficient teachers. They have bungled their handling of the question of teachers' salaries: so much so that the Government had to bring in legislation, the Remuneration of Teachers Act, in order that the Minister should have power to put the Burnham Committee into cold storage for two years so that he could enforce his own pay scales. As Eric Lubbock, M.P., said on behalf of the Liberal party in the debate on the second reading of the Bill (25 April 1963):

'One would think that for such drastic action to be taken the Burnham proposals must have been outrageous. . . . I am not maintaining that the Burnham solution was perfect, but it is worth emphasizing that no negotiated settlement can be perfect, and must always finish up as a compromise which is acceptable to the various interests concerned.'

The basic scale for a three-year-trained teacher which the Minister proposed, £630 rising to £1,250 by fifteen varying increments, is not substantially different from the rejected Burnham proposal of £650 rising to £1,250 by sixteen increments, though the Minister has altered the incremental structure of the scale to give larger increases to those making a career of teaching. The colossal drain of young women does produce acute staffing problems, especially in primary schools, though in the long term the effect could be to build up a very large pool of older married women who can be attracted back to teaching either full or part time. Moreover the Minister has refused to accept the complete assimilation of all two-year-trained teachers to the new scale, which could mean that married women will not return.

The Liberal party has called for the reform of the Burnham Committee to permit independent arbitration and for an inquiry into pay, working conditions, and pensions. It is unrealistic to maintain that the Minister should be excluded from salary negotiation, as he is responsible for teacher supply and especially as the Exchequer through the general and rate-deficiency grants contributes about 60 per cent of the cost of teacher salaries. The Minister, however, has confirmed the bad impression among teachers that through the Government's attitude they will always lag behind the private sector in wage and salary negotiations.

There is a great need to bring fresh ideas and new knowledge to bear on teaching. This must be helped by an expert advisory service. The inspectorate is too busy with administrative routine to concentrate on teaching methods. High teaching qualifications open to all teachers and carrying a salary increment which could be obtained by attending a 'refresher course' and by evidence of first-class teaching on the job would also add a much needed incentive to good teaching. This sort of investment in better and more up-to-date teaching is a national responsibility. The only way to get the teachers the country requires will be to increase substantially the number of university graduates who are available for teaching. The Robbins Report envisages that higher education places will increase by not more than 80 per cent as a proportion of the relevant age group by 1980. This is not enough. Only 'doubling in a decade' will produce sufficiently qualified people to ensure that our children receive the kind of education in the size of classes that they deserve.

Developing All the Talent

Even if Britain adopted a system by which any school-leavers who wished to enter university could do so there would still be a waste of undeveloped talent. As the Robbins Report points out: 'The proportion of middle-class children who reach degree-level courses is eight times as high as the proportion from working-class homes.' This is not because middle-class children are naturally brighter but because working-class children get less opportunity both at school and at home to develop their talents. Their parents are less interested; they leave school earlier. They are often put in lower streams than their ability warrants. Mr J. W. B. Douglas found that in the group of children he studied 11 per cent more of the middle-class children got into the upper stream than would be suggested by their measured ability. Their parents had a car and consequently could make use of a distant school more easily. The working-class boy or girl, however clever, was often condemned to attend a primary school which had been built during the Crimean War – at least 17 per cent of our primary schools have part of their buildings dating back over 100 years – schools which have a low record of success at eleven plus.

This waste continues in the secondary schools. About a fifth of the boys and girls in the group have I.Q.s of 113 and over, yet 15 per cent of that highly intelligent group in the survey had left school by sixteen, and almost four fifths of the leavers were working-class youngsters. Eleven-plus selection must be replaced by a non-selective system of secondary education. It distorts the primary schools' work by encouraging streamlining even from the early age of eight and by crowding such activities as crafts or an oral foreign language out of the last two years of primary school in order that the pupils can be 'prepared for eleven plus'. We know from Dr Douglas's work that manual-working-class children show particularly severe deterioration if they are put in the lower streams. This is also true of children who 'fail' the eleven plus. They become apathetic and decide that education is not for them and cease trying to make anything out of school.

The eleven-plus selection is therefore unjust. Dr Mays of

Liverpool University has shown that the success rate in the eleven plus of the newer primary schools of the suburbs is sometimes as much as ten times as great as that of the depressed schools. Furthermore we know from the example of the countries which have achieved a higher rate of scientific and technological progress that eleven-plus selection can be abandoned without fear of intellectual decline. Having to rub shoulders with their less intellectual contemporaries does not pull down the standards of the brightest children. It is significant that neither the Russians nor the Americans have tried eleven-plus selection, that the Swedes have abandoned it, and the French have put the age of selection up to thirteen. Non-selective secondary education, on the model of the Leicestershire plan, should be supported wherever possible. All children should pass on from the primary school without examination to a common secondary high school. When the child is fourteen the parents should have a free choice whether to keep him at the high school for a final year of vocational training or send him to a grammar school for two years. This system provides the benefits of comprehensive schooling without requiring schools of, say, 2,000 pupils, such as Kidbrook, nor does it necessitate the scrapping of existing school buildings. It also means that streaming in both primary and secondary schools would be unnecessary – in primary schools because there would be no selection examination; and similarly under the Liberal principle of the 'open door' everyone who wanted to would be able to get to a university.

As a longer-term aim the transfer age from primary to secondary schools should be raised from eleven to thirteen. There never was any strong educational reason for making the break at eleven. When the school-leaving age was fourteen it was cleary impracticable to postpone transfer long after the age of eleven. At thirteen-plus children are quickly adopting an adult's outlook on life, and it would be possible to create a different environment in the common secondary high schools if the children were all adolescents. Moreover it would raise the average age of the pupils in primary schools, which would lead to a desirable influx of more men and more graduates. Lastly, it would allow the State primary schools to offer a direct threat to the preparatory schools because it would become much easier for public or other inde-

pendent schools' children to by-pass them and receive their full
five to thirteen education in the State primary schools.

Public Schools

What should be the future of the public schools? One thing is
certain. They should be neither abolished, nor left without any
role in the national pattern of secondary education. Abolition is
unacceptable because parents have the right to send their children
to an independent school if they wish. It must be remembered
that there are nearly twice as many children in independent
Roman Catholic schools as there are in the public schools belonging to the Headmasters' Conference. On the other hand the
survival of privileged education commanding access to the best
jobs cannot be reconciled with equality of opportunity.

On the whole the public schools have high educational stand-
dards. According to a recent survey by the Advisory Centre for
Education, they have a better record than the maintained grammar schools although they do not do as well as the direct grant
schools in the O-level passes in the G.C.E. This is a good record
as they accept pupils with I.Q. range down to 105. Against their
high educational standards and their corporate identity, which
often brings a wider meaning to education, must be set their
defects, in particular the snobbery, the excessive attachment to
tradition, and the complacency their continued existence seems
to bring into English life. It is perhaps not the actual snobberies
of the public-school boy which are so distasteful as the ramifica-
tions for English society as a whole of the existence of an élite
among the young. Public-school values are aped by the State
schools. There are the ridiculous school uniforms which are
worn by children attending some of the seedier London schools.
The public schools are the apex of a social triangle whose very
existence seems to introduce a hierarchical set of social values to
many different aspects of English life.

A Liberal study group has suggested that there are four possible functions for public schools within the national system
which would justify some measure of public support and at the
same time change their class structure. The public schools could
fulfil a valuable social function by providing boarding education
for children who are in need of boarding. It has been estimated in

a report of a working party set up by the Ministry of Education that Local Education Authorities and the needs of the Armed Services could take up between a quarter and a half of the total capacity of the public schools. Children who would benefit from State-assisted boarding education would include orphans, children of parents overseas, children of separated parents, and children whose educational development was being stunted by conditions at home. The Liberal Group suggested that the Ministry of Education might recognize certain schools for this purpose and pay a capitation fee towards the tuition of all pupils as is done in the direct grant schools. Some contributions would also be expected from the schools themselves. The remainder of the fees would be paid by the Local Education Authorities under the present arrangement which exists for paying for boarding at a maintained school and recovering a contribution from the parents on an income scale.

Secondly, some public schools could be transformed into sixth-form colleges, accepting some fee-payers but mainly serving the local authorities by providing comparable sixth-form experience to pupils in rural areas where there is not sufficient population to provide an adequate range of sixth-form courses in a number of small grammar schools. Not every sixth-form college would need to be entirely boarding, and some might be co-educational. Others could be 'country day schools' which keep their pupils on the premises for something like ten hours a day, five and a half days a week.

Thirdly, some public schools – and this group would include the best-known schools – could make a valuable contribution to the national needs through becoming liberal arts colleges or the undergradaute department of a new university. This role would be especially important if everyone left school at sixteen and those who continued full-time education took a general course for two or three years before entering graduate schools – which would largely consist of existing university departments of the older universities.

Further Education

Liberals hold that all young people should attend college for a minimum of three years (while the school-leaving age is fifteen) starting with at least one day a week for liberal studies. In spite of the fact that the Education Act of 1944 provided for universal part-time education to eighteen, only five out of every ten young people get any further education at present. The 1944 Education Act called for county colleges. These are desirable but must await the increase in the overall supply of teachers. In the meantime liberal arts colleges could supply courses of liberal studies for any release students as well as for full-time students.

Further education must be reorganized to meet the needs of a changing society. The aim must be primarily not to prepare people for special vocations but to facilitate their adjustment to innovation and change. In teaching this means showing students 'why' instead of teaching them only 'how'. Care must be taken to ensure that social adjustment keeps pace with technical skill.

The alarming situation at present is that 80 per cent of children still leave school at the first opportunity. Of 270,000 boys who left school aged fifteen in 1962, 122,000 were going to jobs that involved no training or training of less than one year. Of 336,000 who entered employment at 15 and over, 121,500 took jobs involving some form of apprenticeship. Even if all those qualified – there is considerable wastage – this would not be sufficient to meet retirements of skilled manual workers. Meanwhile masses of semi-literate boys and girls are swelling the ranks of unskilled workers, though industry is using fewer and fewer of them.

The country's biggest untapped reservoirs of ability will remain those who missed their chance through leaving school early or through an unlucky choice in their first job. At last the Government is beginning to realize the importance of this problem. But very little will be accomplished as long as medieval regulations bar a man from qualifying for skilled work because at the age of sixteen he chose less skilled work or a craft for which the demand has since fallen off. Nor will the Industrial Training Bill overcome the problem of movement between industries, as it restricts its provisions to tackling the problem industry by industry. This is a national problem which can be solved by the Government exerting the same forceful leadership in this branch of education as it does in others. It requires the setting up of a much-strengthened Youth Employment Service to ensure that all young people, and particularly those who leave at the earliest opportunity, get the best possible choice in their search for employment. We also need forward planning estimates for manpower, nationally, occupationally, and region by region. Lastly, it requires from the highest level to the lowest that everyone should be employed on work that fully uses his ability.

Men and women, whether in the factory, the office, the shop, or the home, should be able to put all their skill and intelligence to work. The limitations of our educational system, our industrial relations, and our present technology make it impossible to achieve this ideal in the immediate future. It is, nevertheless, a goal towards which our sights must be set.

8: Partners in Industry

Britain will never be able to take full advantage of the new technical revolution as long as industrial relations reflect the industrial chaos and social attitude of the nineteenth century. A cold class war is still being waged on the factory floor, which prevents new techniques being adopted. Deep suspicions remain in the minds of trade unionists about the intentions of management. Some of these feelings of insecurity will become more potent sources of industrial unrest as technological changes create more and more redundancies, unless there is a radical change in Britain's industrial relations. We must replace the old prejudices, expressed in terms such as 'we' and 'they' by a sense of common cause.

The government has a positive role to play in stimulating both management and men into a recognition of their common interest; the Ministry of Labour must do more than hold the ring. Under both Conservative and Labour Governments the role of the Minstry of Labour has been to act as an umpire between two medieval armies drawn up for battle. The object of the exercise has been not to prevent conflict but to see that the fighting has been carried out according to the rules of the game. Recently there have been indications that the Conservative Government was realizing that this policy of waiting for trouble could only intensify the 'war'. In 1962 more workers were involved in strikes than in any year since 1926. The Government began to make more progressive noises. In the summer of 1962, after eleven years of Conservative administration, the Prime Minister announced attempts by the Government to formulate a positive policy for industrial relations: 'We must devise measures relating to the status and security of the whole working population, whether on the floor of the factory, in the office or in the shop.' The 1947 Conservative Industrial Charter was taken off the shelf and given another dusting. The Bills which were introduced, however, were the Shops, Offices and Railway Premises Bill, based on the recommendation made as long ago as 1949 by the Gower Committee, and the Contracts of Employment Bill.

Both these measures were watered down as the result of opposition from the employers' federations. The result is that they fall far short of what is needed and hardly make any attempt to catch up on the advances made in other industrial countries. The Contracts of Employment Act, for example, though designed to improve security, provides no minimum period of notice for workers with less than two years' service, which means that the majority in casual industries like construction and ship-building will be excluded from its safeguards. It is the casual industries, however, where feelings of insecurity often cause the most trouble.

The biggest single cause of unofficial strikes in Britain is workers' opposition to redundancy. The Government has admitted that the existing schemes in industry are unsatisfactory. The Minister of Labour, then Mr Hare, said on 9 April 1963: 'Until I have completed discussions with both sides of industry, I do not wish to prejudge the decision of how all the problems will be tackled. The Government is determined that the problems should be tackled effectively. We shall not hesitate to introduce legislation if this is necessary.'

About a year later, in February 1964, it was announced that the Conservative Government had shelved the idea of legislation on severance payments for redundant workers. According to the *Financial Times*: 'The change of plan is understood to have been caused by difficulties encountered by the Ministry of Labour in preparing a redundancy Bill which would be acceptable to both unions and employers.'

Even when a Conservative government wants to introduce positive reform in the field of industrial affairs its hands are bound by the employers' associations and its motives suspected by the trade unions. The trouble is that the employers' associations can be just as conservative and obstructive as the trade unions. Although they were formed for different reasons they have come, as have the trade unions, to adopt a purely defensive role in industrial relations. Most labour disputes, for instance, are sold by the union officials to their members as a defence of traditional union rights. Mr Ted Hill, the General Secretary of the Boilermakers' Society, will not even acknowledge that the phrase 'restrictive practices' is a valid one. He would rather refer to 'the traditional practices of our craft'. But the employers' associations are just as bad, as they also see their role as a purely defensive one – protecting their member companies from trade-union demands. Mr Hugh A. Clegg, of Nuffield College, Oxford, has pointed out that although the engineering unions are 'not generally famous for progressive thinking' they did link their recent pay demands for larger increases for workers on or near the basic rate to a three-year pay agreement. The latter proposal 'was thought to be in line with the views of N.E.D.C. on long-term planning, and the other would have helped to reduce the gap between average engineers' earnings and the industry's extremely low basic rates'. Mr Clegg says the employers rejected these proposals and made no suggestions of their own for improving the industry's wage structure, although they were willing to enter into discussions to consider the implications of long-term agreements. They later conceded a pay increase of up to 5 per cent. Mr Clegg comments: 'Thus the Engineering Employers' Federation has ended up with an apparently inflationary wage increase, which brings them no compensating advantage whatsoever, and they have spurned the progressive proposals of the unions, undoing the work which the union leaders had put in to persuade their executives and conferences to support them.'

Only a radical party which is tied to neither the trade unions nor the employers' associations can have the conviction and determination to sweep away the barriers which prevent Britain bringing its industrial affairs up to date. At the 1962 Assembly, the Liberal party called for the establishment of a National Redundancy Fund. The details of the fund had been proposed in the Report on Industrial Affairs which had been presented to the Party Executive. It proposed a fund to be financed by a contribution from employers and the State which would supplement the national insurance unemployment benefit up to a minimum of two thirds of a worker's average earnings for a period of six months. The provision of adequate redundancy benefits would encourage unemployed men to undergo retraining and move to new jobs. At present unemployment benefit for a married man represents a lower percentage of the average national pay packet than the dole did in 1938. Unemployment benefit has lagged a long way behind the rise in living standards and un-employment for the average worker with hire-purchase commitments represents a graver danger than it did before the war.

Only about 20 per cent of the workers are covered by locally negotiated redundancy compensation schemes. However, the unions have resisted a national redundancy scheme on the grounds that it might encourage employers who have entered into redundancy agreements to reduce their terms of compensation to a statutory minimum. As four fifths of the employed population are not covered by any redundancy agreements this attitude is difficult to understand. Under the Liberal proposals the unions would still have plenty of scope to negotiate above the level of the national minimum.

A Minister of Labour ought to encourage trade unions to negotiate formal contracts of employment which contain certain specified minimum terms, including the requirement that no distinction be drawn between grades of employees in sick pay, leave, or pension arrangements. There is no justification for maintaining differences of principle on these matters between staff and manual workers. Likewise all pension rights should be made transferable. Thirdly, length of notice should be proportionate to length of service, rising from a minimum of two weeks after one year's service to twelve weeks after ten years. At present workers in some industries can be fired at a few hours' notice. Employers should have an incentive to estimate their labour requirements more accurately.

There can be little doubt that 'fringe benefits' have not played an important role in British industrial affairs. According to a nation-wide survey undertaken by Glasgow University the level of 'fringe benefits' expenditure as a proportion of payrolls was more or less static betwen 1955 and 1960. The average expenditure on pension schemes was $2\frac{1}{2}$ per cent of the payroll or a little more than that for canteens. Sick pay was even lower, $\frac{3}{4}$ per cent of the payroll, and redundancy payments, 0.15 per cent of the payroll, was bottom of the list.

Wages have remained the first priority of British trade unions although it is doubtful if the most aggressive trade unions have been able to benefit the relative position of their workers as a result of a national wage increase, as these are invariably

T—D

followed by rising prices. American unions have concentrated more on receiving 'fringe benefits'. A recent example of what they have been able to obtain is well illustrated by the contract signed in 1963 by the United Steel Workers of America with eleven big steel companies. This contract provides for a 'sabbatical quarter' (thirteen weeks) every five years for all long-service employees. This means that men who spend their working lives in steel can expect to enjoy a clear three months' paid holiday before they are 40. Between 40 and 60 a man can look forward to a whole year to spend as he pleases.

The government should lend its help to the wider promotion of 'fringe benefits' linked to a higher productivity by providing information and education. It should draft model schemes. Statutory wage-fixing bodies should be given power to provide for fringe benefits as well as for basic wages. Where it is itself the employer, the government should act directly.

A government ought also to encourage plant bargaining. The conditions of today call for unions representing whole industries and for local branches based on factories rather than geographical areas. Bargaining should be encouraged at company or plant level; this would bring the shop stewards into the negotiations and eliminate the need to manipulate overtime bonuses and piecework ratings in an effort to overcome the difficulties inherent in national bargaining. Much existing plant bargaining is essentially a waste of effort, forced on firms by the need to circumvent the slowness and rigidity of national agreements which should be confined to negotiating minimum rates and to consolidating the position of sectors less able to take the lead. At present much negotiation takes place at an inappropriate level. National bargaining is isolated from the real forms of industrial activity, the factory, and has the inflationary effect of spreading increases indiscriminately, whereas under a system of plant bargaining it would be possible to relate wage increases to productivity.

Plant bargaining would not only mean that the shop stewards would have to be incorporated in the work and machinery of the unions; it would also lead to a better staffing of the middle and higher levels of the union in order that better professional advice could be given to those who bargain at plant level. The members would be more inclined to pay higher dues for extra staff if they could see the practical result in the form of tailor-made agreements to suit the conditions in their own factory.

There are also some trade-union practices which though basically sound have been allowed, through carelessness, to develop in ways which defeat the objectives of the unions to defend their members against arbitrary action. These include dishonest elections, the denial of the right of workers to representatives of their own choosing, and excessive penalties imposed without due process of the law. It would be best for the unions to put their own house in order, though the government should be prepared to pass legislation to give the Registrar of Friendly Societies power to supervise trade-union elections and to investigate cases where a union appears to be flouting its own constitution.

The measures outlined so far would go some way towards creating a sense of partnership in place of the existing industrial struggle. Organized labour and management cannot remain at each other's throats if they are to negotiate and honour guaranteed annual wage agreements covering periods from three to five years. The negotiation of fringe benefits, for instance, will require a new professional approach to industrial affairs, on the part of both management and the union officials. Collaboration on these matters would lead to a new appreciation for the role and rights of both sides. Yet it is equally necessary that a sense of partnership is extended beyond the union official to the employees. Partnership in industry will remain a slogan until employees are given a share in the decisions and the profits of the companies in which they work. The established employees of all public companies should have a legal standing in the company. There are many ways in which the participation of the employees in the running of their companies can be fostered. One step is effective joint consultation with works councils representing all grades, and giving greater responsibility on all matters affecting the interests of the employee, including the introduction of profit-sharing and employee shareholding schemes.

To complete the structure of formal participation, the Companies Act should be amended to give all established employees in public companies a status similar to that of shareholders. The Liberal Yellow Book of 1929 recommended the establishment of a supervisory council consisting of elected representatives of both the shareholders and the employees, to which the Board of Directors would be responsible. This is one possibility. Another method of achieving greater participation by the employees would be through the election of worker directors. Since shortly after the First World War employees in German industry have had a right to statutory representation at both a works council level and on the Board. The German works councils discuss a wide range of decisions, including what in British practice would be negotiating as well as consultative matters, as well as a number of major questions of management policy on questions involving, for instance, the closing or transferring of a plant. The Works Constitution Law of 1952 entitles the works councils to appoint a third of the Board's members although only two belong to the firm. In the coal and steel industries the employees under the co-determination law of 1952 can appoint full board members. The shareholders appoint another five, and the two groups then elect a neutral 'eleventh' man. The normal practice is for the shareholder group to nominate the Board Chairman while the employee group nominates the 'eleventh' man. Of the five employee members two come from the trade unions, and two from within the firm; and the fifth, though also nominated by the unions, must not himself be involved in either the firm or the union.

The effect of electing one third of the board as employee representatives has been nominal. They have some influence, but they can be and commonly are kept away from the real seat of power through management meeting as a steering committee. On the other hand the results of equal representation in the coal industry have been quite striking. There has been a substantial gain in industrial relations, above all in mutual understanding on the part of the trade unionists, executive managers, and shareholder representatives.

The successful results from equal representation in the German coal and steel industries have been helped by the special situation of these industries in the boom years of the 1950s. Further, the unions have been able to find a good supply of qualified candidates to serve on the boards because there has been a limited number of companies to service. Thirdly, the post-war situation produced an environment in which both unions and management were open to new ideas. The unions were outgrowing their class ideology, and the management had been impressed by the human relations movement in America. Lastly the entrepreneurial initiative of the executive managers has been strengthened rather than weakened by the team efforts which have resulted from the various forms of representation. The German co-determination experiment encouraged the Liberal Party Committee in its Report on Industrial Affairs to suggest that minority representation of employees in any representative body was not enough. On the other hand the Committee felt that the unimpaired responsibility of management for executive action was imperative. Effective participation did not require that worker-directors should necessarily sit in on board meetings. The answer, the committee considered, lay in the establishment of an Annual Representatives' Meeting composed equally of representatives of shareholders and of employees to replace the annual general meetings of limited liability companies. Of course, it does not follow that because the German experiment in co-determination has been relatively successful in the German coal and steel industries it could be helpful in Britain. The sceptic, indeed, may well ask at this stage if, had there been any genuine demand for participation on the part of British employees, would not the trade unions already have pursued legislation on the German pattern. The answer to this question is that British trade unionists are paying increasing attention to employee participation schemes abroad. A high-level delegation, including Mr Cousins and Mr Woodcock, has visited Germany and Yugoslavia to investigate the operation of their schemes. More and more informed people in the field of industrial affairs are realizing that the only alternative to negative control by the unofficial strike is positive participation on the part of the employees.

There have been some notable success stories among the British companies which have experimented with employee participation. A Liberal study group has investigated the kind of participation operating in British industry following the debate of the Industrial Affairs Report at the 1962 Liberal Assembly. One large motor company with an excellent history of industrial relations has a Management Advisory Council consisting of

twenty-two elected representatives and six management representatives. Employee members are elected directly from the shop
floor on a one-man-one-vote basis. In the elections an 80 per
cent poll is normally achieved. The twenty-two elected members
are nearly all unionists, including ten to twelve shop stewards.
The term of office is three years, and continuity is preserved by a
third retiring every year. About two thirds of the elected representatives make service on the Management Advisory Council a
full-time job. The management regards this as a good and cheap
investment in trouble-free labour relations. The employee representatives for their part seem to consider that through the
Council and its sub-committee they can influence decisions in
nine cases out of ten. The representatives also place much emphasis on the direct lines of communication they have with top
management; trouble can be brought to the notice of management and a settlement reached in a matter of hours without
reference to union branch committees. It is also interesting to
note that official company recognition in wage bargaining is
restricted to dealing with two unions; furthermore although
there are 275 shop stewards accredited to the company, they
play second fiddle to the twenty-two elected representatives.

The company also attaches great importance to the selection
and training of supervisors. There is vocational training for both
foremen and shop stewards. Those chosen go into the company's training school and receive a six-month sandwich course
including instruction in industrial relations; and on the successful completion of the course every effort is made to fit the men
into a supervisory post immediately.

A few progressive companies are already embarked on extensive programmes of employee consultation. In some cases the
personality of the moving spirit behind the original development
has played a large part in getting the participation securely
adopted. The chairman of a small engineering company investigated by the Liberal group had pressed through a scheme
whereby an employee who is elected as chairman of the works
council becomes a full director and performs the functions of a
personnel manager. Another large retail organization has a central council where at least two thirds are elected by the employees.
The council, in turn, elects five members of the central Board.

Questions like the fixing of minimum pay rates, cost of living adjustments, closing times at public holidays, the practicability of the shorter working week, and so on are referred to the central council which is often, in effect, left to exercise the power of decision.

Progressive managements have found that the acceptance of change is more painless where there is an opportunity for participation. The men most interested in participation are usually those employed in jobs making greater technical demands than the average. Mr Banks, in his interesting case study of a Unilever subsidiary,* found that the managerial implications of a post of some authority carry a social status far outweighing any of the technical or economic aspects of the job, and similar conditions apply to voluntary officers. He suggests that the achievement of status based on technical proficiency – having a part with a high job rating – inspires a desire for status in the social sense and hence an interest in voluntary office.

Banks also found that it was the New Men – the men with greater knowledge and experience of a company's processes who were employed in jobs ranking higher than average in skill, responsibility, and mental requirements – who had an interest in voluntary office. Furthermore he found that the more there is a general upgrading of skill combined with a tendency for smaller working groups arising from technical change, the greater the extent of participation on the part of the work force. This is an extension of earlier findings of the Liverpool University investigation that the greater the amount of participation by workers in decisions about change, the greater the speed with which change is assimilated.

For the British worker, the welfare state has proved – as Michael Shanks has pointed out† – in many ways a cruel sham: 'He is still as far away as ever from achieving a real partnership of power ... indeed in many ways class barriers have become more rigid in recent years while each class blames the other for the country's failure to advance socially and economically.' There has been no attempt to lay the foundations of a genuine

* J. A. Banks, *Industrial Participation: Theory and Practice – A Case Study* (Liverpool, 1963).

† *Encounter* (July 1963).

partnership by either Labour or Conservative governments. This must be started in the factory – it cannot be superimposed from above. Opportunities have been lost again and again because the union leaders, the employers' federations, and the Ministry of Labour have immersed themselves in the details of industrial relations. Because the union leaders, the employers, and the State have been trying to settle a host of plant details through national bargainings they have left themselves little time and energy to think freshly about the general lines of the pay structure, for example, by revising ancient skill differentials or ending unequal pay for women or reforming the trade-union movement itself. The Ministry of Labour with its large staff and resources has not been able to cope with both the broader issues which should be its proper concern and the fiddling detail in which it has too often involved itself. Still less can the small overloaded and under-paid staffs of the trade-union national offices cope with these.

British trade unionism will never be right until it is given the climate in which to reform itself. The Conservatives have completely failed to create the right environment. Since 1951 the unions have devoted themselves wholeheartedly to pressing for higher wages precisely because they felt free to do so in the ac-quisitive society which the Conservatives favoured. 'In a free for all,' Frank Cousins remarked, 'Labour is part of the "all".' The Conservatives have completely failed to convince the workers that their interests can be properly safeguarded in any partnership established by a party with the connexions and history of the Tories. It is true that a substantial section of the working population has been voting Tory since 1951. This is not, how-ever, because they felt that the Tories will give them any share in a partnership of power. It is the result of the feeling of frustra-tion and disillusionment which swept over the working class after six years of Labour austerity had failed to give them any real sense of participation in society. As the Labour Government had failed to turn a capitalist society into a socialist one, they felt they might as well vote for a party which claimed that it knew how to make a capitalist society work.

This is no longer so. The failure of successive Conservative Chancellors to lay the basis for a steady expansion of the British economy, the pay pause, and the cynical way in which the

Conservative Government has tried to put the blame for its own economic policies on the trade unions has forfeited most of the working-class support. Will this now return to the Labour party? It is true that the trade-union movement still officially recognizes the Labour party as its political own. A Labour M.P., Mr Loughlin, frankly admitted this to be the case in the House of Commons on 25 June 1963 when he said: 'The trade union movement recognizes that the Labour party continues the industrial struggle in the political field. ... The unions, both nationally and through their branches, have consistently paid into Labour funds for that purpose.' Fortunately more and more people are recognizing that the industrial struggle will never be won so long as the gulf between the minority ruling clique and the majority working mass remains unchanged.

9: Security in a New Society

When so much needs to be done in our society it is intolerable that the energies of the trade unions should be concentrated on fighting phoney issues and that their objectives should be so terribly limited. Since 1951 real average earnings have risen by less than 50 per cent – an annual gain of 3½ per cent compound which does not begin to compare with the rise in the value of equity shares which have more than doubled in the same period. In spite of the fact that money weekly earnings have doubled the real gain has been only half as much and the unions have not managed to win a larger share of the national income; their share has remained at a little over 42 per cent over the 12½ years of Conservative government.

The rise in wages has not worried the manufacturers who, in the absence of competitive conditions, have been able to pass on the increase to the consumer by way of higher prices. The net effect has been a steady inflationary push which has benefited the Stock Exchange and company directors but has adversely affected the fixed income holder, and especially old people. The attitude of the Conservative Government to the old-age pensioner has been especially cynical. In every election manifesto they have made pledges to 'ensure that pensioners continue to share in the good things which a steadily expanding economy will bring' (1959); knowing full well that the low level of State benefits combined with rising prices has meant hardship and deprivation for many old people.

The present standard rate for retirement, sickness and unemployment benefit is 67s. 6d. a week for a single person and 109s. for a married couple. But national average industrial earnings are over £16 a week. This means that on retirement, sickness, or unemployment there is a reduction in income of about two thirds. This is a very sharp fall in the standard of living of the family concerned and forces more and more people to seek help from the National Assistance Board. When it was set up in 1948 the Board was envisaged as a temporary stop-gap which eventually a rising of the level of prosperity would leave with nothing to do. Today, under the Conservatives, it has become the central prop of the national social security system. At the end of 1963 more than two million people were on national assistance, which is the highest since the scheme started. Between one quarter and one fifth of all pensioners have to supplement their meagre pension with national assistance. Recently a survey by Mr Peter Townsend of the London School of Economics indicated, however, that at least twice as many people live at or below National Assistance level as those who receive it.

The first priority in social security is to fix the basic level of pensions and other social security payments high enough for people to live on them without National Assistance. The function of social security is no longer simply to prevent starvation but to offer protection from deprivation and help towards the steady maintenance of the standards of living earned by work in times of sickness, unemployment, or retirement.

The way to guarantee the basic level neither need nor should be the same in the case of all benefits. Guaranteed minimum pensions should be provided by raising the flat rate State pension over a period of years high enough to make a married couple's pension equal to half the average weekly industrial earnings of an adult man. At the present level of earnings this would be £8 a week for a married couple and £5 a week for a single person. Once the basic pension had been raised, nine tenths of those now dependent on National Assistance would no longer require this help, and the National Assistance Board as such would come to an end. Provision for the remaining tenth would continue, although this would now come from a Ministry of Social Security. Secondly the earnings rule must be abolished. Pensions should be payable at retirement age on qualification by citizenship or residence after five years with no retirement conditions.

Whatever the level of pensions in the first year of retirement, it should be adjusted upwards from year to year with the rise in the average industrial earnings. Pensioners cannot be left behind by the rest of the community. It is completely unreasonable to have old people with only the income which was adequate at the date of their retirement. This unfortunately is what has happened to the public-service pensioners under the post-war governments. Meanwhile in the private sector salaried employees can look forward to a 'dynamic' pension. The managers of pension funds today in many big companies invest a large percentage of their funds to ensure adequate pensions at the date of retirement. More and more are also using equities to guarantee dynamic pensions rising after the date of retirement.

The government ought also to encourage employees – through their trade unions and professional organizations – to supplement their State pensions by private occupational schemes to a level of at least two thirds of previous earnings. Everybody should have a chance to make supplementary provisions in this way, and the government should compel employers who do not have an occupational scheme to contribute to a government-run fund to offer employees this chance. The present Conservative State Graduated Pensions Schemes should be withdrawn. It is a bad bargain and was originally introduced to increase the level of contributions in order to meet the large expected deficit in the national insurance fund. A young man aged eighteen earning £15 a week and paying 5s. 1d. to the graduated scheme on top of the 11s. 8d. stamp would get a much higher yield (about $2\frac{1}{4}$ times as much) if the same amount were invested in a private scheme.

Unlike the Labour party, Liberals believe that occupational schemes must be encouraged. While the State must plan and supervise the whole framework of provision and ensure that both the public and private schemes are adequate, it should not have a monopoly. If social security is to operate in the future as it has done in the past, it must go on operating through independent as well as State agencies, with as many openings for initiative and progress. The new standards of social security which have arisen since the Beveridge Report have been put into practice because of firms, professions, and individuals who have been free to try new ideas and back them with their own resources.

The Labour Pension Plan is likely to squeeze out many of the voluntary occupational schemes. The success of the whole plan depends on a large number of higher-paid employees being in the State scheme. As Mr Crossman has admitted: 'Labour's scheme will be one which it will be very expensive to contract out of.... We shall make a great many conditions.'

The Labour party favours all pensions being State-financed because it proposes to use accumulated pension funds to buy up large holdings in industrial equities as a means of achieving investment targets and getting companies to follow national plans. This approach is to be rejected. National investment must certainly be planned, but there are better ways than by forcing non-socialists, in the course of providing for their old age, to finance a programme for bringing more and more of British industry under socialist control.

The best way to finance voluntary occupation schemes is by funding. Contributions paid in advance build up for each contributor a capital fund. As the fund accumulates interest over a period of years the direct cost to the contributor need only be half what the final fund will be worth. When it comes to financing State pensions, however, there are several reasons why funding is not a good method. The existing national insurance benefit is paid for not out of contributions already paid out by current pensions contributions. Each younger generation finds from its pockets the pension of its fathers and grandfathers and in time hopes to be looked after out of the pockets of the next generation. If national pensions were to be entirely funded people now working would be paying both in advance for their own pensions and financing the pensions of their parents. A pay-as-you-go method of financing is the simplest way of arranging that the lower-paid workers do not have to pay the full cost of their pensions out of their present limited earnings. This would be best arranged by a social-security tax assessed on the basis of each company's payroll, subject to a ceiling, and charged two thirds to the employers and one third to the employees. This percentage social-security tax would replace the present flat rate national insurance stamp plus Exchequer contribution.

At present the British employer pays a much smaller direct contribution than in other European countries. The British practice of wresting about half the cost of social security out of general taxation is a direct encouragement to employers to hoard labour, and a disincentive to capital investment. Whereas in 1961 in Germany every additional worker employed meant an extra 1s. 8d. per hour in security charges, in Britain the cost was only 8d. Financing social security by a payroll tax would put the whole cost of welfare on the employer and the employee. It would also become obvious to all concerned that when they voted for higher pensions they would increase the social-security tax proportionately. As the basis would be pay-as-you-go it would be possible to have regional variations in the level of contributions. In congested areas, such as the south-east of England, it would be possible to have a higher level of employers' contributions than in the north. This would help to make labour more expensive in areas where there is already an over-concentration of employment. Employers would have a strong incentive to plan future developments in the less congested regions. Finally, the revenue available to the State would rise automatically as earnings go up. This is not the case at present with the system of flat-rate insurance stamps. Under the present system it would be neither just nor politically possible to raise the extra money needed for adequate social-security benefits by charging more and more into the stamps, as the lower-paid workers already pay a sizeable proportion of their wages towards national insurance.

A further necessity is an earnings-related sickness and un-employment benefit scheme guaranteed by the State, and giving a minimum of two thirds of what is earned while at work. Above this level, employees should be encouraged to negotiate through occupational schemes for 100-per-cent benefits through the first months of sickness or industrial retraining. The experience of other countries shows that benefits representing three quarters or more of earnings are no more than is required to avoid sharp breaks in the standard of living.

Once the general level of insurance benefits had been raised to a respectable level for unemployment pay – the present rates for a single person are just over 20 per cent of average earnings – there would be no need for the national redundancy scheme already outlined, which Liberals have pressed for as an emer-gency measure. All operatives, clerical workers, technicians, supervisors, and junior managers would be covered by the scheme, which would be financed by the social-security tax. Other salaried staff would have to look to company schemes for earnings-related benefits. On the other hand, there would be a ceiling to either the contributions or the benefits under the State

scheme for unemployment and sickness benefits as these would
be related to individual and not average industrial earnings. The
ceiling could stand at twice the average earnings of adult male
industrial workers. Contributions would be payable and benefits
calculated only in relation to income falling below this line.

Firms and industries would be encouraged to provide for
the first weeks of sickness or unemployment. This both maintains
a worker's human ties and puts pressure on his firm or industry
to minimize sickness or unemployment and the cost arising from
them.

The Liberal plan for social security would transform and
simplify the role of the Ministry of Pensions. First the whole
machinery of stamps and individual contributions would be
abolished. The State pension would be paid at a standard flat
rate to all those who could prove they were over 65 (or widows
over 60) and were either British citizens or had an approved
period of residence. Secondly the very complicated Conservative
graduated pensions scheme would be swept away, and the even
more complicated Labour proposals would be avoided. With
its burden of detailed administration reduced, the Ministry
would be free to concentrate on its main task: to formulate
national policy for social security and see that it is carried out in
the private and occupational as well as in the public sector.

The Ministry of Social Security would encourage the development and expansion of voluntary and occupational schemes by
drawing up model schemes and indicating essential minimum
requirements; by encouraging fringe benefits on an industry-
wide scale by giving statutory wage-fixing bodies the power to
provide these benefits; and by setting a good example in the
public sector. Under the Pensions Increase Act of 1962 the
pensions of teachers and civil servants who retired in 1951-2
still fall short by margins of 15 to 25 per cent of those who
retired in 1960-1. The Liberal party proposes to review public-
service pensions every two years to keep them in line with the
increases of those still in work.

A central fund would be set up to provide for employees not
covered by approved occupational schemes. Every employer not
running a satisfactory pension scheme would have to contribute
to this fund. Any employee without an adequate pension would

be allowed, if he chose, to save up to a given percentage of his earnings in a retirement annuity with an insurance company or a friendly society and have his contribution boosted by the central fund, thus increasing his pension. If those methods of encouraging voluntary schemes should fail, however, the Ministry of Social Security would consider making participation in occupational schemes a requirement for all employees. This would be done only after industry had been given a period of years to put its own house in order. From the outset it would be a condition of approval of a pension scheme by the Inland Revenue that all private pensions are transferable between jobs, including the benefits which accrue through the employer's contributions. This is a serious obstacle at present to economic efficiency and individual freedom which often ties managers to jobs they would otherwise leave. It would be disastrous if similar ties were extended to the whole working population.

The Liberal aim is to enable everyone in need or in retirement to receive two thirds of pay through a combination of the national insurance benefit and an occupational scheme. By these means it will be possible to overcome the problems of providing high earnings related benefits for all. As *New Society* commented when the Liberal plan was published in *Security in a New Soviety*:

> Undoubtedly the most interesting feature of the new scheme is its handling of the division between State and occupational schemes. Perhaps the most imaginative solution so far to a problem which has concerned policy-makers of all parties . . . The Liberals neatly get round all these difficulties by providing the basic pension through the State (officially above subsistence level) and virtually compelling occupational schemes to take the level of benefits further. The central fund proposal, to which employers who will not or cannot introduce schemes must contribute, gives all employees hitherto favoured the chance to provide for themselves if they so wish. No one can complain if they end up only with the State minimum.

This working partnership between a State security scheme and occupational schemes drawn up by individual firms and industries keeps the taxation required to finance the benefits within bounds. Because a substantial part of the amount spent on improved social-security schemes would not pass through the national budget but through occupational schemes the Liberal party scheme would not fall so heavily on the taxpayer as the Labour proposals. Unfortunately the finances of the Labour proposals have not been published this time. When their original plan, *National Superannuation,* was published in 1958 Mr Crossman admitted that the detailed costing figures in it were 'shot to pieces'. The new proposals contained in *New Frontiers for Social Security* avoided this risk by omitting all calculations of this sort. There can be little doubt that it would put a much heavier burden on the taxpayer than the Liberal scheme. It has been estimated that the Labour pension proposals alone will take 13 per cent of the national income; the addition of sickness and unemployment benefits will raise the cost to about 15½ per cent. The Liberal plan would cost between 11 and 12 per cent and would be introduced over a transitional period of seven years.

One must not underestimate the cost of introducing earnings related to benefits on the scale envisaged in *Security in a New Society.* This is a massive task but nevertheless one that must be done in a country with a rapid rate of growth. The alternative is to accept growing inequalities in our society. Unless the elderly, the rich, the widows, and the lower-paid can be offered the kind of benefits to which salaried employees have become accustomed there will be a growing division between those who benefit from a national policy of growth and those who lag behind. The Conservative party believes that it will be sufficient if the social benefits go only to those who cannot stand on their own feet. This is a mistaken policy: social security is not poor relief. It must be part of a national policy for a dynamic society; a means of integrating the working population into a national partnership by offering everyone the right to participate in the benefits of schemes which at present are obtained only by top people through 'top hat' schemes.

10: Britain's Role in the World

Britain and Europe

Britain emerged from the Second World War depleted in resources but with the prestige of victory and the trappings of a great power. Only Liberals seemed to have realized that whereas the war had been won, Britain had lost her independence of action. In the event, Labour and Conservative foreign policies were dominated by the past to such an extent that they failed to grasp the opportunities which presented themselves to Britiain in the post-war years.

The years after the war presented Britain with an enormous challenge. There were great global upheavals such as the emergence of the new nations, the dominance of the American and Soviet blocs, and the revolutionary changes in communications and trade as a result of technological progress. These changes were vital to Britain's role in the world. It should have been transparently obvious that our future no longer depended on our ability to maintain the 'imperial lifeline' of world bases built up in the days of the first industrial revolution. Britain's power then was based on coal and on the navy with its fuelling stations round the world connecting the biggest empire in history, from which we were able to draw cheap food and raw materials and also the exhilarating sense of being top nation. The war had forged deep bonds with the Commonwealth and the United States, but Britain is and has long been part of Europe; she cannot live without Europe nor Europe without her. The post-war years witnessed a remarkable change in Europe's position in the world. Two great powers, Russia and the United States, had emerged as the major power blocs, and the former great powers of Western Europe had shrunk in relative importance. It became increasingly obvious to the leading statesmen of Europe that if they were to defend their interests and take advantage of the new technological revolution they must overcome the limitations of their own resources and national sovereignties.

Some politicians in the Labour and Conservative parties did recognize that Britain, for all its links across the seas, might achieve a more important and significant role in the world if she took the lead in establishing a new partnership of nations in Western Europe. But even Sir Winston Churchill, despite his prophetic vision of the need for a Franco-German *rapprochement*, always thought of Britain as associated with a European grouping and not part of it. Britain, he pointed out, was the meeting place of three great circles – Europe, the Commonwealth, and the American alliance. He did not believe that Britain should take the lead in the movement towards European unity nor did he hold that modern technology had removed the *raison d'être* for the nation state.

It was left to the Liberal party to urge upon the Labour Government the wisdom of a foreign policy whose primary aim should be to strengthen the bonds between this country and the rest of Western Europe. In 1947 the Liberal Assembly called upon the Government to consider what steps should be taken towards a United Europe by setting up agencies to pool resources in specific sectors. When M. Robert Schumann proposed in 1950 that 'as a first step in the federation of Europe' the entire Franco-German production of coal and steel be placed under a common High Authority open to other European countries, Mr Clement Davies, leader of the Liberal party, hailed the Plan as 'the greatest step towards peace which has ever been taken' and called upon the Labour Government to take part with others in working out these proposals for the benefit of all.

The Labour Government was not prepared to accept either the political objective of the European Coal and Steel Community, as it was called, or the transfer of control over the British coal and steel industries – which was limited largely to matters such as the coordination of trade policies which membership of the new organization required. The Labour politicians felt that the Western European politicians had a parochial view of the world as a whole. The Labour party was engaged on a much grander exercise – the transformation of the Empire into a Commonwealth of Nations. As the leading nation in the Commonwealth, Britain, it was felt (by Labour and Conservative parties alike), remained a great power.

The Commonwealth idea played an important role in giving the Labour party a feeling of international purpose when it was becoming more and more nationalistic. Mr Michael Young, who should know, as he was head of the Labour Party Research Department during the period 1945–51, asks the question in his pamphlet *The Chipped White Cliffs of Dover*: 'Has not the Labour Party always been internationalist?' His answer is: 'Certainly it was until the war. But from 1939 on a change has set in. The war and the power that followed it seemed to have shrunk the Labour Party not just into a nationalistic party, but more into a Little Englander Party. Witness Labour's attitude to Europe both before and after 1951.'

On the continent, by contrast, very different forces had been at work. When the war came to an end France was still smarting over the humiliation of 1940; Germany was a stricken country scarred with blitzed cities; Italy's pathetic nationalistic dreams had proved an ugly farce. These bitter experiences utterly discredited the idea of the nation and brought home to the continent of Europe that the world had changed. To this desire to unite M. Jean Monnet brought the realization that the future lay with regional groupings of countries who could pool their resources and take advantage of modern technology and large-scale production. Monnet had spent the war years in Washington as the French representative on the team in charge of coordinating the task of mobilizing the Allied war effort. So the attempt to unite Europe was a combination of an economic desire to take advantage of what the future had to offer combined with a determination to lay down political foundations which would frustrate another war between the countries of Western Europe. At first the continentals still hoped to carry Britain with them. Both France and Germany wanted to have Britain as a counterbalance to the possibility that either of these two countries might dominate the new Europe. But Ernest Bevin insisted that the only form of European cooperation which a Labour Government would support was an inter-governmental arrangement which would only progress as fast as the slowest member wanted to travel. When General Marshall made his dramatic offer of a massive aid programme to get Western Europe back on its feet it was Mr Bevin who insisted that the Organization for European Economic Cooperation (O.E.E.C.) should be an inter-governmental body whose secretariat could only initiate proposals which had been agreed to by all the member countries. In the years of reconstruction it became obvious that the British Government wanted to travel painfully slowly along the road of European Cooperation. The six countries of Western Europe which later formed the Common Market determined to go ahead with a pilot project designed to pool resources under a supranational umbrella. This was the European Coal and Steel Community, which Labour rejected as too vague and contrary to its own ideas about national economic planning.

The European Coal and Steel Community was a great success. In 1955 a conference was held at Messina to decide on the next step towards European unity. Once again the British Government – this time a Conservative Government – was invited to take part in the discussions, once more they refused to. An Under-Secretary for the Board of Trade was present as a British observer at the original Spaak talks which led up to the drafting of the Rome Treaty but he was withdrawn by the Government when the discussions changed from a technical examination of the problems involved to a negotiation on a plan of action. The only reason for this blunder can have been that the British Government calculated that the Common Market would never be ratified by the French Assembly. This was not the first time the Conservatives had miscalculated the strength of the European movement. On the last occasion the proposed European Defence Community collapsed because the British Government was unwilling to participate.

Meanwhile the Rome Treaty began to take shape and the Conservative Government had to explain away its failure to participate. The three principal arguments put forward to defend the Tories' decision not to join the Common Market were the Commonwealth, British agriculture, and the supranationalism involved in the Rome Treaty. Already the good faith of any British Government was in doubt on the continent. The Europeans had noticed that although the Commonwealth was made the pretext for holding aloof no attempt was made to consult the Commonwealth partners: they were merely informed of our decisions. The suspicions were, if anything, reinforced by the attempts made by Mr Maudling to link the Six with a European Free Trade Area. It looked to some Europeans like an attempt to get into Europe without paying the subscription. The Six showed their objections by insisting on two conditions: that the Free Trade Area must be surrounded by a common external tariff and that it must include agricultural as well as industrial products. The negotiators haggled fruitlessly until General de Gaulle, now back in power, sent them packing.

Conservative miscalculation and double-talk did considerable harm both within the country and outside. A tendency towards ambiguity – some would call it duplicity – on the part of Mr Macmillan towards most matters, and in particular towards the European Economic Community, did not help. It started as soon as he achieved power as the champion of the Suez diehards: he promptly proceeded to do the opposite of all they expected. In foreign affairs, however, the Government must ensure that the ground is well prepared before there is any drastic change in policy. They must give a lead. But neither Mr Macmillan nor Sir Alec Douglas-Home has been able to give the country a lead for fear of antagonizing his own right wing.

The 1962 Commonwealth Prime Ministers' Conference was a reminder of the harm done by a Conservative Government through its initial mistake about the Common Market. Tory double-talk also delayed the preparation of British agriculture for any negotiation with the Six. In an attempt to scare potential Liberal votes in the West Country before the General Election Mr Maudling is quoted in the *Guardian* as saying on 5 November 1959: 'We never dreamed of joining the Common Market. If we joined it we would have to abolish all tariff protection for agriculture and horticulture and give up control of our own agricultural policy. This would mean an end to agricultural price reviews and the Acts of 1947 and 1957.'

If the Government had been making use of these years to prepare and not scare British agriculture from entry into the Common Market there would not have been the concern there was in 1962 among farming circles and Conservative backbench M.P.s about the change-over from a deficiency payments system to a market support system. The mechanics of the 1957 Act were breaking down in any case. In spite of an increase in the subsidy bill from £206 million in 1955/6 to £343 million in 1961/2, farmers' real incomes during the last ten years have fallen and food prices in the shops have gone up by over 15 per cent. Today the 1964 Agricultural and Horticulture Bill has gone a long way towards the Common Market system. Even the Labour party has adopted a programme of establishing a Cereals and Meat Commission to manage the market (which had already been proposed by the Liberal party) as a means of introducing a system of market price support rather than, as at present, through guaranteed prices which the farmer receives no matter at what price his produce is put on the market.

Mr Macmillan also engaged in a dangerous piece of double-talk concerning the political implications of the Rome Treaty. Mr Butler, for instance, said at the 1962 Conservative Conference that 'the present negotiations do not take into account the question of political union'. Mr Macmillan was a little more honest when he admitted at Llandudno that the Treaty of Rome 'has its political implications'. 'But', he hastened to add, 'while close cooperation is involved there is no question of our being asked or expected to accept any system of a federal character involving the sovereignty, in the true sense of the word, of the Crown and Government and people of these islands.'

The European Economic Community, whatever top Conservatives say to the contrary, is not a purely economic venture. Professor Hallstein, the President of the European Economic Commission, has said:'We are not in business, we are in politics.' Liberals want to see the Economic Community develop into a political community through the evolution of a pragmatic and gradual development of the community method of operation.

Mr Gaitskell at the 1962 Labour Conference raised another bogey: that Britain inside the Community would be reduced to the status of the State of Texas in the American federal system. This would not be possible under the Community system as evolved by the Six. The Common Market was built on the conception of give and take, of partnership between the members. The Labour patry seems unable to think in new political concepts. The Treaty of Rome is not a cut and dried constitution for a Federal Europe. It is a framework of action. This can be most succinctly expressed as essentially a dialogue between those who speak for the Community – the members of the Commission – and the spokesmen of the national interests. The key to the success of the Community is first that there was a political impetus behind it and second that there is a high-powered commission of experts whose job it is to prepare proposals whose recommendations can be either adopted or rejected, but not amended, by the Council of Ministers of the member countries. There is no attempt by the Commission to use its powers of initiation to steam-roll proposals against the wishes of important interests. On the contrary, as the Commission desires to have its proposals accepted by the Council of Ministers, it does not usually put forward proposals without a long preparatory process of consultation and modification.

The Conservative double-talk about the political implications of the Community and the emphasis the Tories had placed on the danger to British agriculture and the Commonwealth during the Free Trade Area talks did not help the negotiations which started in the autumn of 1961; with the result that they dragged on for more than a year. Having previously raised many objections to the Rome Treaty, the British Government could hardly start negotiating by accepting the main obligations of the treaty. Nevertheless it was quite obvious that the Six were prepared to make only minor exemptions and protocols to suit our special position. When the Treaty was drawn up, agreement was reached by making decisions about the main points and leaving the details for further negotiations. If the Government had accepted this procedure the negotiations would have gone much more smoothly. Further, it would have been advantageous if the Commission had played a leading part in the negotiations from the beginning; however, the British Government seemed unwilling to call in its service. Lastly, to the surprise of the Six, the British took up a rigid position on domestic agriculture. This position was opposed by all the Six countries from October to December 1962. The Six felt that what the British asked made excessive inroads into the new common agricultural policy they had devised. The Conservative Government must have known that France in particular would bitterly oppose any major change in the E.E.C. agricultural policy, which affected its most sensitive economic interest. The only reason which explains the British attitude is the pressure which the Tory backbench M.P.s were bringing to bear on the Government from the rural constituencies.

The Labour Party Conference at Brighton also played a part in bringing the negotiations to a halt. Mr Gaitskell came out strongly against the Common Market in an effort to unite the party before the General Election. As the influential *Washington Post* commented at the time: 'The voice still seems to be Gaitskell's but the words sound more like Lord Beaverbrook's.'

The Labour party case was based largely on three objections. First, that economic planning was incompatible with the Rome Treaty. But as Sam Brittan, the economics editor of the *Observer*, pointed out:

It seems fantastic that the British Labour Party has failed to see that the Commission is not only the political spearhead of the Common Market but also the biggest driving force in the Western world towards full employment and social welfare. If Labour were seriously concerned with constructive economic planning it would seek to strengthen the commission's hands instead of delaying its supranational features.

The Labour party also opposed the Common Market on the grounds that as Britain still exports twice as much to the Commonwealth as it does to the Common Market we should not risk losing our Commonwealth markets for the sake of joining the E.E.C. The fact is that the Commonwealth preference system offers this country no alternative to the Common Market. Mr Gaitskell tried to counter this argument by pointing out that 85 per cent of British exports to Australia get a preference averaging 10 per cent. He did not add that it is in Australia where the decline in the British share of the market has been greatest. In the period 1954–60 our share of the Australian market has fallen by 21 per cent. According to Messrs Gilbert and Major, who made a study of Britain's falling share of sterling area imports in the *National Institute Economic Review* for March 1961, the evidence pointed to preferential margin having a stifling effect on initiative and enterprise in our Commonwealth markets. The Commonwealth countries are not prepared to remove their tariffs towards British exports which protect their developing industries. The Common Market, by contrast, would have given British industry an increased home market of at least 170 million more consumers in return for opening up our domestic market of 52 million. Moreover the Common Market would, unlike the sterling area markets, not be liable to be closed off suddenly for political reasons or as a result of a balance of payments crisis.

Mr Gaitskell's fatal performance at Brighton did not go unnoticed in Paris. It seemed that there was now no chance that the Labour party would accept the terms being negotiated by Mr Heath. 'It's no use negotiating with Mr Macmillan,' President de Gaulle is reported to have said to the Italian Foreign Minister after the Rambouillet meeting in December 1962, 'he is finished politically.' The final straw which undoubtedly made up de Gaulle's mind was the Nassau agreement. At Champs in June 1962 he was reported as being pleased with the Prime Minister's suggestion that when Britain came in it would move on towards a common European effort in defence. He probably expected the Conservatives to pool resources in the field of nuclear weapons. Mr Thorneycroft had, after all, prepared the ground with the European space club and cooperation in the aircraft industry.

Britain's nuclear future was brought to a head in December 1962 by the American decision to drop Skybolt. Mr Macmillan went to Nassau and, after five days of bargaining, he obtained the Polaris missiles as a substitute. It was true that the Nassau agreement on Polaris was designed to lead to a multilateral N.A.T.O. deterrent and that President de Gaulle was invited to participate. But Polaris was an American weapon and President de Gaulle regarded the existing set-up in N.A.T.O. as mere camouflage for American domination. Mr Macmillan was, in de Gaulle's eyes, committing Britain's nuclear future to the American alliance. Although the British Government now decided to compromise over agriculture and the negotiations were just about to reopen President de Gaulle suddenly announced that Britain would be an American 'Trojan Horse' in Europe. A few days later he broke off the negotiations.

The Deterrent

The Gaullist veto on British entry into the Common Market has left all the countries of the Atlantic alliance, with the doubtful exception of France, without a strategy for the West. In particular the Conservative Government remains in a state of dazed confusion. Having made one of the biggest volte-faces in political history, it still finds it difficult to believe that the door has been slammed in its face. Sir Alec Douglas-Home, it is true, has leapt with alacrity into the breach with his 'war cry' of the British Deterrent. He has worked hard to try and convince the electorate that the British nuclear striking force still gives Britain a 'special relationship' with the United States; though his arguments sometimes sound more like an attempt to convince that the V-bomber force gives us the right to put pressure on the Americans through a not very subtle form of nuclear blackmail.

It is true that there was a time – about in the middle of the 1950s – when the Americans did accept the V-bombers as fulfilling a complementary role to the Strategic Air Command in so far as the R.A.F. with its speed and proximity to the Russians could be in action faster than the American bombers. At that time the British Government no doubt had a 'hot line' to Washington, and it could be argued that, at moments of crisis, the British Prime Minister could bring pressure to bear on the American administration.

These days have gone for ever. As everyone knows, at the time of the Cuba crisis, when we all came nearer to nuclear destruction than we have ever done before, the V-bombers did not even entitle us to listen in on the exchange between President Kennedy and Mr Khrushchev, let alone influence the American President's course of action. One reason is that in spite of repeated warnings that 'limited national nuclear armaments are dangerous, expensive, prone to obsolescence, and lacking in credibility as a deterrent' (McNamara on 16 June 1962) and that 'the British nuclear effort over many years has strained available resources, reduced conventional forces to a minimum, and produced a nuclear capability that may be perhaps 2 per cent of the nuclear striking power which the United States could now bring to bear on the N.A.T.O. area' (Mr Dean Acheson, *Foreign Affairs* 1962), the Conservatives have steadfastly refused to stop pouring millions down the drain and strengthen our conventional forces. The result is that in so far as there is any special relationship today in the Western Alliance it is probably between the Americans and the West Germans who are supplying the bulk of European conventional forces within the N.A.T.O. alliance.

The insistence of the Conservative party on the need for

Britain to maintain independent control over the V-bomber force has instead created a crisis in the Atlantic alliance. As Mr Aubrey Jones, a former Conservative Minister of Supply, pointed out in the House of Commons on 26 February 1964: 'If one has an alliance with more than one centre of nuclear decision, each looking with suspicion at what the other will do, I do not believe that that alliance will last. It will crack, as, I believe, the Western Alliance is now doing. It is cracking. That is why I do not believe in the indefinite co-existence of interdependence and independence.'

Even before the 1959 General Election, when the Labour party was still advocating that Britain should retain the nuclear deterrent, Liberals were advocating that Britain should give up her independent control of the V-bombers by integrating them in the N.A.T.O. alliance. At the same time Mr Grimond insisted the British Government must press for reform of the alliance structure so that N.A.T.O. should be so organized that each member nation should, through joint consultation and mutual coordination of policies, be in a position to exercise some political control over the use of the Western deterrent, thereby reducing the risks of unilateral action and contributing towards the 'collective security' of the West. If steps had been taken in the late fifties in this direction it is quite possible that General de Gaulle, when he returned to power, would not have embarked on the *force de frappe*. He has put forward claims for a French independent striking force largely to gain access to and exercise some influence over the development of American strategic policy.

The existing N.A.T.O. machinery has the double disadvantage of making the European powers anxious and uncertain about American strategic capabilities and intentions and of obscuring the factors which may force them to modify their own defence policies – to maintain, for example, a higher level of conventional manpower and equipment if technological and other factors are making dependence on nuclear weapons too dangerous a policy to meet the whole range of contingencies which may confront the alliance. The Americans, who could have been convinced about the need for a greater degree of political control in N.A.T.O. by the British Government in the fifties, now argue strongly in favour of a centralized command structure on account of the introduction of the missile into the strategic balance. The speed of nuclear missiles has compressed the time margins available for political decisions from hours to minutes. As Mr Buchan has also pointed out: 'The anonymity of the missile immediately inculpates the largest power in any alliance, no matter whose national emblem may have decorated the one fired against the adversary. The unchallenged penetration of the missile makes it necessary to deter its use by the adversary through the development of a second-strike capability which sets a premium on complex and expensive systems for achieving invulnerability on numbers of units of strategic delivery, on areas of low population density, on warning time, in short on exploiting the assets which the United States happens to possess and Europe does not.' (*Foreign Affairs*, July 1963).

The American administration, for the strategic reasons given above, and because it is wary about negotiating individually with a number of countries much weaker than the U.S. within the alliance, made it quite clear in the Nassau communiqué that the U.S. was reasserting the need for a centralized American strategic system. At one time the Kennedy administration had hoped that the movement for European unity meant not just the emergence of a European Economic Community but a political system with which they could share their nuclear strategic responsibility. These hopes were dashed by the failure of the Conservative Government to negotiate entry and by President de Gaulle's action in breaking off the talks.

Instead the American administration has revived proposals on which its officials have been working for some time for a N.A.T.O. seaborne force, largely to satisfy the growing feeling on the part of the West Germans that if Britain and France have nuclear striking forces they should not be left out. The N.A.T.O. seaborne force will have three elements: three American Polaris submarines which will be assigned to N.A.T.O. from the American fleet; the four or five British Polaris submarines (when they are commissioned towards the end of the decade); and twenty-five missile-firing surface ships belonging to N.A.T.O. itself and manned by mixed crews from those powers in N.A.T.O. who wish to participate with the missile warheads in the custody of an American team. By this means the Americans say that the

European nations will be able to acquire a greater sense of participation in strategic policy, and in particular Germany will be in a stronger position to resist French blandishments for Franco-German nuclear partnership.

But in fact neither the multi-lateral force of surface ships nor the Polaris submarines is an adequate solution to the control of strategy within the alliance. The force itself is marginal to the strategic requirements of the West, and consequently represents no real shift of the American burden to Europe, while it obscures the question of control. The European countries would be buying – at considerable expense – only a safety catch on the American trigger on a fraction of the American strategic forces. If the other European governments, especially the West Germans, decide however to go ahead with the multi-lateral force then the British Government should also lend its support for political reasons. It would certainly be a mistake to oppose as the Labour party propose, and also foolish to vacillate as the Conservative Government has done. But the West needs a new initiative – this time from the European side of the Atlantic.

Only a partnership between the United States and Europe can avert the dangers which will confront the Atlantic alliance if it is left to drift without any positive direction. The United States cannot propose a viable partnership because the American Constitution expressly states that the American President cannot share sovereignty with any other nation. The U.S. Government also cannot relinquish her veto on the use of nuclear strategic weapons except by legislation, which Congress is unlikely to accept if it is initiated from the American side of the Atlantic.

Britain must take the initiative in pressing for greater political control of the Western deterrent before the United States and Europe begin to lose confidence in each other. The first step must be to offer to integrate the V-bomber force into N.A.T.O. without reservations of political or military independence. This revolutionary step would create the necessity for fundamental reforms in the structure of N.A.T.O. itself. At present the alliance is merely a collection of national units. The result is every nation can veto any decision taken by the N.A.T.O. Council. Secondly the secretariat, unlike the Common Market

Commission, cannot prepare policy papers unless unanimous agreement has been reached by the relevant countries.

It is because N.A.T.O. is so indecisive that Mr McNamara is loath to place more policy decisions in N.A.T.O. hands. On the other hand the European countries might not agree to a more decisive form of organization unless they felt that they were more deeply in the confidence of the United States planners. This vicious circle will be broken only by a major initiative such as the irrevocable handing over of the V-bomber force – and any Polaris submarines which Britain may have by that time. Britain would then be in a position to insist that N.A.T.O. decision-making was made more effective. In particular we could call for the creation of a powerful civil-military secretariat, akin to the Common Market Commission, which would be capable of putting forward an Alliance point of view – through effective joint planning – rather than just the aggregation of the sum of individual national plans. This would end the divorce which at present exists between political discussions in the N.A.T.O. council and military planning in S.H.A.P.E. and Washington. We would also be able to call for weighted voting and majority voting on certain issues. In particular the problems of credibility, the safety catch, and the trigger would have to be tackled by a N.A.T.O. nuclear executive which could be composed of the United States, Britain, France (if she agreed to integrate her nuclear force), and two rotating members. The weighted voting could be so arranged that the United States could be out-voted only by all the Europeans voting together.

The Americans would retain physical control over their own strategic weapons but the United States would have to accept joint consultation and the mutual coordination of strategy regarding the use of Strategic Air Command in respect of the N.A.T.O. area and consultation in respect of the S.E.A.T.O. and C.E.N.T.O. areas. As the techniques of control were evolved, however, there would be growing pressure on the Americans to accept that S.A.C. should also be brought within the orbit of N.A.T.O. rather than be directly responsible to the President of the United States. The situation arising from the British initiative would also call for the development within N.A.T.O. of a European Defence Authority from which a more coherent

European voice on military and strategic questions would gradually emerge. The advantages of a European Defence Authority would extend from the common production of weapons down to the integration of all land forces to divisional level with common logistics. At present defence planning within N.A.T.O. has been bedevilled by the multiplicity of types of aircraft, tanks, guns, and missiles. It has made the whole Western defence effort unnecessarily costly and greatly reduced the flexibility of the N.A.T.O. commanders. For instance, there are in the central area of Germany alone seven types of three-ton trucks in use. Only an integrated defence production system is going to allow the British military aircraft industry to keep in production. The enormous cost of the TSR2, about £2½ million per plane, is accounted for by the small numbers that the R.A.F. can order. The Americans can produce the TFX much more cheaply because the American Air Force is ordering 3,000 – against the 120 TSR2s ordered by the R.A.F.

Obviously the whole of our aircraft industry would probably not be able to maintain its existing level of production: there would have to be even greater specialization than at present. However, the production runs would be large enough to make it possible for unit costs to be significantly lower than at present, which would benefit the taxpayer and our export industry.

The most important reason why N.A.T.O. must be faced with an initiative of this kind as soon as possible is that in less than five years time the North Atlantic Treaty will have to be considered in any case. After that time, that is twenty years after the original agreement, the signatories can withdraw from their Treaty obligations. This means that there are only a few years ahead in which to decide what form the political structure of the alliance will take in the 1970s. If, moreover, the objection to any British initiative is that France would not agree – this might well be the case in the first instance: but in view of the fact that the N.A.T.O. political structure will have to be overhauled in any case (and if France objects she might have to withdraw completely from N.A.T.O.) it would seem that French agreement is not impossible, especially as many of the advantages of joint political control of the Western deterrent have long been sought by General de Gaulle.

If there are doubts about whether Britain should agree to integrate the V-bomber force in N.A.T.O. without reservation, it is only necessary to consider the arguments put forward by the Conservative party to be persuaded otherwise. The controversy about the British independent deterrent stems from differences of view about the future role of this country in world affairs. On the one hand there is the Conservative party, which believes that we must cling to nuclear independence as the last means of hanging on to the shreds of nineteenth-century grandeur, and on the other hand there are those, like the Liberals, who want Britain to develop a new leverage of influence through twentieth-century cooperation with our allies in a Western defence system.

Since 1957 when Mr Duncan Sandys decided to put the emphasis on the *British* nuclear effort, Liberals have pointed out (long before the Labour party) that the British independent nuclear deterrent was unnecessary as it only duplicated the American Strategic Air Command. The Government argued that the V-bomber force was a credible deterrent because by itself it was enough to make a potential aggressor fear that our retaliation would inflict destruction beyond any level which he would be prepared to tolerate. The Government's case here has always rested on doubtful assumptions. It assumes that in the event of an attack our V-bombers are likely to escape destruction on the ground. All too probably a surprise attack, which is presumably what we are trying to deter, would eliminate most of Bomber Command before its planes were in the air. Even if a few surviving aircraft were able to take off it is doubtful whether the number that could get through to their targets would be sufficient to 'inflict destruction beyond any level which a potential aggressor would be prepared to tolerate'. Doubts have also been expressed about whether the V-bomber force is not already obsolescent. According to a Staff Report on *Problems and Trends in the Atlantic Partnership,* presented in America in October 1962, the V-bomber force was 'already approaching obsolescence' at that date. It is true that Mr Hugh Fraser, the Secretary of State for Air, announced in February 1964 that 'Bomber Command will remain an effective force for many years to come; ... far from waning it is growing.' This announcement was made precisely one week after the American Government had demoted the bombers of the powerful Strategic Air Command to second place. 'Although most of the aiming points in the Soviet target system could be best attacked by missiles, the long-range bombers will continue to be used for follow-up attack,' said Mr McNamara. The British V-bomber force, however, has no missiles to follow up and many experts believe that it is precisely because Britain has none that the life of Bomber Command is being extended to 1972 at a cost to the nation of not less than £2,000 million. As the *Economist* reported at the time of Mr Amory's announcement: the V-bombers 'are not to be withdrawn, and only last week they made an appearance in a new guise, as ground-level attackers that would notionally fly under the level of Russian radar cover to launch a missile some 100 miles from a potential target. One may doubt just how effective this suddenly discovered new function for the V-bombers could really be. But what is certain is that this new function has been devised only in order to maintain the possibility of entirely independent nuclear action by Britain.'

The 1964 Defence White Paper justifies the independent nuclear deterrent on different grounds from those used in the 1962 White Paper, 'that the V-bombers could inflict destruction which a potential aggressor would not be willing to tolerate'. This time the White Paper says:

To suggest that the independent deterrent might be abandoned in the interests of non-discrimination overlooks the fact that if there were no power in Europe capable of inflicting unacceptable damage on a potential enemy he might be tempted – if not now then perhaps at some time in the future – to attack in the mistaken belief that the United States would not act unless America herself were attacked.

This argument depends upon a doubtful thesis. It is that an enemy might try to attack the European partners of the N.A.T.O. alliance while declaring it had 'no further territorial claims' on the United States of America – unless a European partner has an independent deterrent. But this argument is not only a justification for Britain having a deterrent. It is a direct incitement to other European countries to get their own independent deterrents. It is the case for a French deterrent – and a Franco-

German or West German deterrent. For the enemy could equally say that he not only doesn't intend to attack the United States but furthermore he does not intend to attack Britain, he intends to attack only Western Germany.

This point was made in the Defence Debate in the House of Commons on 26 February 1964 by Mr Aubrey Jones, the former Minister of Supply. Mr Jones went on to point out:

'I ask the House to reflect: is it in the military interests of this country to have in the Alliance more than one centre of nuclear decision? It is perfectly true, as my right hon. friend the Minister of Defence said today, that if any enemy – say the Soviet Union – were to attack Western Europe or this country we, by threatening the use of nuclear weapons, could force the United States into nuclear hostilities against her own will. We could, to use the jargon, act as a catalyst. But – and this is the point – by the same token, if there is more than one centre of nuclear decision within the alliance, others can act as a catalyst against us too.'

Nuclear proliferation is the greatest danger in the world today and the arguments used by the Government and the Prime Minister are a direct nuclear invitation to other countries to develop their own nuclear bombs – no matter how ineffective they are – so long as they could involve either the United States or Russia in a war for which they would otherwise have no stomach. Sir Alec Douglas-Home, for instance, said in a speech to a Young Conservative Conference on 15 February 1964: 'If it is the nuclear bomb which has kept and is keeping the peace we must have the bomb.' But world security is so greatly weakened by the refusal of the Government to give up its claim that Britain must have independent control of its deterrent. Suppose the West Germans accepted the arguments used by the Government in its recent White Paper and linked themselves to the French deterrent; is it not possible that a situation could arise where the French and Germans would want to take a tougher line than the British and would use this nuclear blackmail in an effort to drag in the rest of the Western Alliance?

This situation is much more likely to arise than any possible set of circumstances where Russia would menace Britain without at the same time menacing a 'vital interest' of the United States that would call into play an American counter-threat, whether or not Britain had an independent deterrent. Any threat by Britain to use its V-bomber force independent of the American striking force would be far-fetched, as it would immediately result in a Russian counter-threat which, if it materialized, would result in the extermination of the British Isles. Sir Alec Douglas-Home seems to have at the back of his mind the nineteenth-century idea that if Britain is attacked at least we shall sell our country 'dearly'. Unfortunately this quaint notion is quite meaningless today: there would be nobody left to wear that particular battle honour on their flag.

The Conservatives also sometimes pretend that the British V-bombers could defeat a non-nuclear power if it threatened a 'vital' area of British concern such as the Kuwait oilfield or Borneo. This point was disproved at the time of Suez. To defend our oilfields with nuclear weapons would be useless and inconceivable, especially as it might also invite Russian retaliation.

Sir Alec Douglas-Home's other argument is that 'nuclear weapons give us influence and authority in the councils of the world' (16 January 1964) and that 'the sole result of abandoning our nuclear arm would be that Britain would not be able to sit at the top table when matters of nuclear policy are discussed between East and West' (3 February 1964). This claim is simply untrue. It was disproved at the time of the Cuban crisis. The only conference the Bomb has ever got us into was the Test Ban Conference in Moscow. It is a most extraordinary argument that one must keep nuclear weapons so that one can be at conferences to make treaties to ban them. Liberals have also opposed the British deterrent on the grounds that Britain could not afford to keep a whole range of defence missiles in various stages of development and employing half of our scientific manpower. To keep up with the arms race a country must not only be prepared to spend vast sums on research and development but must also be ready to write off large sums as and when the circumstances require. This Britain clearly cannot afford to do. Yet whereas America and Russia have not increased their defence budgets this year the British bill has gone up by £161 million and will rise more steeply if we go on pursuing the chimera of an independent deterrent.

In the nuclear and missile age that followed the Second World

War it became clear to anyone who was not blinded by nationalism that technology is challenging the whole foundation of national sovereignty. Only powers with enormous resources of skilled manpower and raw materials can remain in the top class. There are only two nations – America and Russia – which can afford the immense sums which must be spent on research and development to keep up with the arms race. It should have been obvious to both Labour and Conservative governments that changing technology demanded radical rethinking about Britain's role in the world. Instead the decisions about the manu-facture of the so-called British deterrent have taken place with the minimum of public discussion either in or out of Parliament. Whereas in America there is a continuous debate of defence and strategic considerations at a high level, in Britain discussions are confined to a narrow circle of specialists centred on the Institute of Strategic Studies. Defence debates in the House of Commons are among the most sparsely attended.

Yet from the beginning of 1950 to the end of 1963 it is esti-mated that the Government has spent £1,200 million on the independent British deterrent. Security provides a useful excuse for preventing everyone from discovering precisely how much of this astronomical government expenditure on the deterrent and other missile projects has been wasted. The Conservative Government has admitted to millions spent on major cancelled programmes. Unofficial estimates, however, have put the cost to the nation of these scrapped weapons at more than £600 million. Whatever the exact figure, it is clear that a nation the size of Britain cannot afford to have something like half her scientists in the service of a very few defence industries, especially as research and development on defence projects has become more and more specialized with less and less application for any civil purpose, let alone the other industries and public services equally essential to survival.

It can be argued that the use of procedures developed in America, such as systems analysis – a scientific method of calcu-lating the relative cost and effectiveness of various weapons systems – could have helped to avoid some of the worst defence blunders. It is well known, for instance, that Blue Streak was obsolete before it was ever started. For political reasons it was built under conditions which 'could only be described as a mess'. Nevertheless, no matter how well the research stage of Blue Streak had been handled, to carry on its development and production would still have cost nearly £500 million more; and the estimates to continue the programme and bring it into service by 1963 were of the order of £6,000 million.

The abandonment of Blue Streak by the Government should have brought home the fact that Britain cannot afford to finance the independent research and development necessary to support an independent nuclear policy. But the response of the Conservative Government was the announcement that Britain was negotiating an agreement to buy Skybolt, the American airborne ballistic missile, which was expected to come into production in 1965. It was hoped that Skybolt, with its projected range of 1,000 miles, would extend the operational life of the V-bomber force into the 1970s. When Skybolt was abandoned because this project was proving much more expensive than the Americans had originally estimated, and it was becoming increasingly apparent that it would be late in delivery and possibly not as efficient and reliable as had at first been hoped, Mr Macmillan met President Kennedy in Nassau in order to try and save the British independent deterrent by keeping Skybolt. Instead the Conservative Government had to accept the Polaris missile as the means by which the fiction of the British independent deterrent could be maintained.

The result of the Conservative search for national grandeur is that Britain is now committed to spend at least £400 million over the next few years on the construction of five Polaris submarines. As only about two submarines will be at sea at any time the absurdity of the situation is immediately obvious. Secondly these submarines will be equipped with American Polaris missiles. It is unlikely that the American Government would go back on its promise to supply these missiles but as part of the Conservative case depends on the possibility of America going isolationist the missiles cannot be taken for granted. Thirdly at the moment the Polaris submarine is undoubtedly the best available second-strike weapon. But no one can be sure that this will still be the case in the period 1968-75 when the Polaris submarines come into service. Mr Maddox, the Science Correspondent of the *Guardian,* has pointed out that the detection of nuclear submarines will not always be as difficult as it is at present.

If the Government really believed that Britain's role in the world depended on the British independent deterrent they would have taken steps to allow for the possibility that Polaris will become obsolete and have included research expenditure for its successor. This has not been done. Indeed, Lord Jellicoe, the First Lord of the Admiralty, let the cat out of the bag when he said in a prepared speech in the House of Lords on 17 March 1964 that:

> I do not wish now to claim that it would necessarily be right for this country to wish to retain this ultimate nuclear option for all time. There might – it is not inconceivable, in my view – come a time when the organic structure of the Western Alliance was sufficiently strong for us to be able with entire confidence to place our nuclear armoury irrevocably in a common pool.

Six years too late the Government are admitting that the Liberal party has been right!

The Armed Forces

The bankruptcy of the Government's defence policy was clearly exposed by the strain placed upon our conventional forces by crises simultaneously in Malaysia and Cyprus at the beginning of 1964. The troops that went to Cyprus were drawn from the central strategic reserve. Their departure left it no longer an organized force but a collection of isolated units, many of them seriously short of men. It also necessitated withdrawing units from the British Army of the Rhine, already gravely under strength. This is the inevitable result of spending large sums of money on a nuclear striking force which will have no value to the nation and little to the Western alliance as a whole.

The first priority must be to bring the strength of the British forces in Germany up to four fully equipped divisions – about 75,000 men – instead of the three weak divisions we have in Germany now. At present the British Army of the Rhine can lose itself in the stretches of the Westphalian plains, where it has an operational task based upon a force of at least twice the size of the existing force. The result is that B.A.O.R. must rely upon the early use of nuclear weapons. This is contrary to N.A.T.O. strategy and could spark off another world war. Alternatively if the political arguments against the use of tactical nuclear weapons prove to be overriding the choices left will be withdrawal or defeat.

If Britain wants to have a voice in the affairs of N.A.T.O. we must not only provide four divisions at full strength in Germany but we must make sure that they are fully equipped. At present only three out of the seventeen battalions of infantry in the First British Corps are mounted in a wheeled troop carrier with a limited cross-country performance. The other fourteen battalions still rely on lorries which are road-bound and entirely restricted to fast-moving fluid operations. Yet modern infantry cannot live on the battlefield today without the protection of armoured vehicles capable of carrying infantry across country under heavy fire within striking distance of the enemy.

The out-of-date equipment of the British armed forces, which have been starved as a result of the resources squandered on the deterrent, has not helped the recruiting figures. The strength of the army rose by 1,500 in 1963 but 8,000 more are needed to reach even the official target. *The Times* Defence Correspondent quotes a young infantry officer in Germany as saying that the newest piece of equipment in his unit was the fruit machine in the sergeants' mess. It is often said that Britain will not be able to meet all her military commitments in Europe and other parts of the world unless she reintroduces some form of conscription. It must be realized that there would be numerous problems attached to the introduction of any form of compulsory selective service. The White Paper of 1957 stated that 'the only really practical form of selective service would be a ballot', but there is no guarantee that a small conscript force chosen arbitrarily by ballot would be suitable for filling the most serious gaps in the Army. Moreover selective service would mean that there would have to be a considerable number of soldiers devoted purely to training the recruits. In effect it might become necessary to maintain an army of perhaps 190,000 in order to have 180,000 effective men – which would greatly increase the cost of the army in terms of pay, food, clothing, housing, and movement. More could be done to make the army attractive to the infantrymen, drivers, doctors, medical orderlies, and specialists in electronics and modern weapons systems, of whom the shortages are grave enough to restrict the employment of formations in battle. For instance, more men would be willing to learn a trade in the Services and serve a number of years in the forces if they were able to practise their trade in civilian life.

Class consciousness is a crippling factor in army life as it is in English society as a whole. There is not only the great gulf between the fighting and the servicing units but, as Mr Cyril Ray remarked in the *Spectator* on 17 November 1962:

There is also among the fighting units themselves the gulf between the fashionable and the dreary, for the snobbery of the mess is often reflected in the barrack room's intake from the recruiting office. . . . I have long thought that the much sentimentalized 'regimental spirit' has disadvantages to balance its very real advantages. . . . I have an idea that the recruiting figures are better for the Navy and the Air Force than they are for the Army, partly, at any rate, because an engine-room artificer and an aircraft hand wear the same sort of uniform and badges and belong to the same unit as the watch-keeping officer and the pilot or air-gunner. . . . My own suggestion is that the various service corps should be disbanded; that every regiment should have its own 'tail' of fitters and drivers and signallers and storekeepers, with the regimental badges up, and enough of them to be pooled for divisional and corps troops.

A review of Britain's overseas commitments is essential in order to get a better deployment of our armed forces. The strategic necessity of maintaining overseas bases is one problem, the military usefulness of these bases, assuming they are necessary, is another. Greater use should be made of the United Kingdom and the overseas bases as the framework for a system of air-transportable strategic reserves and joint service task forces built round Commando services and flat carriers. This will require a strong balanced fleet and large numbers of aircraft for the transport and offensive support of ground forces in limited operations of war. The U.K. Strategic Reserve consists of an infantry division, a parachute brigade, and aircraft of a Royal Air Force tactical group which provides air transport – long- and short-range – and close offensive support for the ground forces. It is, however, badly under-strength. One of the three brigades is only a planning headquarters with no troops permanently available to it. There is a shortage of administrative and signal units. Only the parachute brigade is up to strength. There are not enough transport aircraft and there is no properly designed fighter-ground attack aircraft for close support. If the Strategic Reserve was brought up to full strength and relieved of its present need to train for continental as well as 'brush fire' war, it would be the ideal conception and organization for limited war forces outside Europe. At the same time priority would be given to the production of transport aircraft and to a fighter-ground attack machine with a vertical take-off and landing performance.

Keeping the Peace

With a full-strength Strategic Reserve it would be possible to withdraw progressively British garrisons from selected overseas garrisons which are already undermanned and are, in any case, of limited utility in the event of an emergency. In the Far East, for instance, the garrison in Hong Kong is at best a hostage to Chinese good intentions: it is proposed to reduce the strength of the garrison there to the equivalent of four infantry battalions for internal security duties. This will make two major units and a number of supporting troops available for duty elsewhere.

In general our policy in south-east Asia, after the present crisis in Indonesia has been settled, should be to encourage our allies in the South-East Asian Treaty Organization, and those countries in the area not so far committed, to take an increasing share in the defence of the area. The eventual aim would be to remove land-based British troops altogether from the area and to contribute to collective defence there mainly through mobile strategic reserves and joint service task forces; but at the same time to take a full part in the military planning and training activities of S.E.A.T.O. The base at Singapore will probably be needed for most of the 1960s to support naval task forces. In any case it is at present essential to a thriving economy on the island. The long-term aim, however, will be to seek in cooperation with the Australian government support facilities in Australia. A small contingent, however, will be contributed to the Commonwealth Strategic Reserve in Malaya until the new policy of mobile reserves is fully effective.

In the Middle East the ideal arrangement for securing our supplies of Middle East oil, which is our main strategic interest, would be on a 'good customer' basis. To achieve this will call for a radical reappraisal of the aims of foreign policy in the area.

Liberals have strongly opposed the existing proposals for a federal state for Aden and the Federation of South Arabia as they consider this policy is being forced on the majority of the population and has the support of only the Sheikhs. Aden should first become self-governing, and then it would determine its own future. Until this is achieved political instability in the area will make it essential for us to maintain a military presence. The development of the Aden base would be continued, and it is proposed to negotiate to keep forces permanently stationed there. The climate of the area makes quick reinforcement from the U.K. impractical. It is therefore planned to strengthen the force by transferring to Aden the brigade from Kenya as soon as political developments in East Africa make it possible. Further reinforcements in an emergency will be by means of the joint service naval task force which will be maintained east of Suez.

The main British commitment in the Mediterranean and the Near East is Cyprus, where we maintain the main base for the air-strike force in support of C.E.N.T.O. This base, however, is of limited value for operations in the Persian Gulf, as became evident in the Kuwait crisis (the only contribution it could make amounted to a handful of signallers and a parachute battalion used as normal infantry), and if its value as a base is doubtful, its security is equally uncertain, as the recent strife in Cyprus has shown. Once the crisis in Cyprus is settled the Sovereign Base Areas should be handed over to a U.N. force, if it is found necessary to keep a truce force on the island; if not the base should be handed over to the Cyprus government and all troops withdrawn. It may be necessary to make arrangements with the Cyprus government for maintenance of certain radar and wireless installations on the island and in that case a small security garrison will be needed.

The recent events in Cyprus have also shown up the weakness of the United Nations as a peace-keeper. The immediate requirement of the U.N. Secretariat is a highly qualified military expertise. The establishment of a small military general staff at the U.N. would provide the nucleus round which a permanent U.N. peace-keeper can be built. At present the peace-keeping forces will have to be drawn from national forces, and the creation of a well-equipped U.K. strategic reserve trained to tackle 'brush fire' operations would provide the kind of force which will be required. On the other hand there is a great deal to be said for the building up by the U.N. of a permanent force with its own bases and supply system. The U.N.E.F. in the Gaza strip could well be developed into such a base. It is all very well for Mr Wilson to talk of giving the British Navy a U.N. role; this kind of proposition seems to go down well among a part of the British Labour party which seems to have inherited the Victorian British 'nannie' complex.

What is really required is a force which owes allegiance to the United Nations itself, and Mr Wilson has been at pains to emphasize that under a Labour government British forces would be 100 per cent under the control of the Labour government. (How Mr Wilson reconciles this attitude with the proposals for assigning the V-bombers to N.A.T.O. has never been explained.)

A United Nations Peace Force with its own permanent headquarters and staff organization could play an invaluable role in preventing smouldering situations in the world from catching fire and dragging in either the Americans or the Russians. It could also develop into a World Police Force which will become necessary if an international arms control agreement can be agreed upon by the U.N. disarmament conference.

Defence policy must be developed in harmony with disarmament objectives and not in direct opposition, as has recently been the case with the Conservatives. The day after Mr Butler made a speech pressing for a number of cardinal points, including the freeze of strategic nuclear delivery vehicles, at the Eighteen-Nation Disarmament Talks on 25 February 1964, the keel was laid in Britain of the first of the five new Polaris submarines. If disarmament proposals are to be taken seriously there has to be compatibility between their development over a period of time and the plans of the defence forces. Mr Thorneycroft, the Defence Minister, speaking in the debate in the House of Commons, on the day after Mr Butler had given his blessing to the American proposal for a verified 'freeze' of strategic vehicles carrying nuclear warheads, including anti-missile missiles, said that 'there is no question and no proposal whatsoever that the United Kingdom should in any circumstances forgo the five Polaris submarines'. There are some signs that the Russians may be prepared to give favourable consideration to the American proposal for a verified freeze of nuclear weapons, but quite clearly they are not going to do so if Britain is to demand the right to an exemption which will allow it Polaris missiles for its five nuclear submarines. And clearly the British Government is getting the worst of both worlds if it frustrates any agreement to create nuclear stability through its insistence on an independent deterrent which can only encourage the spread of nuclear weapons, and, in the long run, make world disarmament very much more difficult.

The development of a U.N. police force would also make possible the creation of nuclear-free zones in areas where there are at present no nuclear weapons, for example Asia, the Middle East, Africa, and Latin America. This would mean that the United Nations itself would have to adopt a more positive role in the world. At present the U.N. Peace Force operates only with the consent of the parties directly concerned, including the government of the country in which it is stationed. It has also limited enforcement powers and does not shoot except in self-defence. But each successive operation has stretched the rules to deal with new factors. So far it has been possible to justify the necessary action in terms of the U.N. Charter. As the Secretary-General gets greater resources at his disposal, however, there will be mounting pressures to strengthen the United Nations itself in order that the 'nascent' world government can play its necessary role in the world. Liberals have always stressed that before the U.N. can be made into an embryo world government we have, in Mr Grimond's words, 'to do some humbler but rather exciting things first – and their key-note should be people working – not only talking – together'. Slowly, on the basis of practice and precedent, the old-world structure of national sovereignty is being eroded. But the process will be accelerated if such a country as Britain is using influence to establish a world order under the auspices of the United Nations.

11: Towards a Welfare World

The Commonwealth in 1964 is not much more than a network of personal and institutional arrangements which links Britain with the old Dominions and the developing countries of Africa and Asia. This network gives Britain a unique place in the world situation, which could provide a positive impetus to world development but has hitherto been overlaid by a haze of after-dinner rhetoric. The positive feature of the Commonwealth arrangement is that as a colonial power Britain, willy-nilly, has involved her former dependencies in a world-wide economy and given them their first push towards modernization. The defect of the present set-up is that Britain has now withdrawn from most of the territories, often in a hurry, leaving them in most cases without widespread education, growing industry, or productive farming. Independence within the Commonwealth finds the developing countries caught between the colonial world from which they have just emerged and the modern world of industrialized nations which they find it very difficult to enter. No situation could be more potentially explosive.

The developing countries of the Commonwealth can be kept in the world economy if they can get capital and skills exported to them at low or no cost and if an international economy can be created in which this capital and these skills can be at least to some extent earned. The need for these countries is markets. Britain, by herself, cannot provide these markets – nor could the old dominions – even if we could persuade them to open their doors to the semi-manufactures of the developing countries.

Mr Harold Wilson is engaging in a dangerous kind of double-talk when in one month he tells the House of Commons (during the renewal of the Commonwealth Immigration Act) that 'We are not discharging our duty to the Commonwealth until or unless we take adequate steps to increase the flow of economic aid to those areas and to expand Commonwealth trade ...' and sends a letter at the Dundee by-election pledging Labour to continued restriction of imports of jute from Pakistan. More recently he has said in the House of Commons (6 February 1964) that we should ask for a specific preference in awarding contracts to Britain from the Commonwealth. As Mr Grimond pointed out: 'We cannot look at this matter as a sort of aid-to-Britain movement. If the Commonwealth can get better and cheaper goods elsewhere than in Britain, it is not very useful to a poor and underdeveloped country to say that it must get them from here.' What neither Labour nor the Conservatives have faced up to is that aid, to be effective, needs above all continuity, and it will be continuous only if it is coordinated through discussion and administration on a joint basis with the other aid-giving countries. Aid to the developing countries will be successful only if each of the wealthy nations will assume its proper share of the aid burden.

Some of the members of the European Community have a much better aid record than the U.K. The 1960 figures for the share that aid to developing countries represents of their gross national product were as follows: France 2.5 per cent, Netherlands 2.13 per cent, Great Britain 1.36 per cent, Germany 0.93 per cent. The Six are already contributing one fifth to the third Indian five-year plan, whereas Britain is contributing only one twentieth of the total. In spite of the fact that almost half the 1.25 billion people in the underdeveloped countries receiving Western aid are members of the Commonwealth we have been contributing only about half as much as France, which has a special interest only in the 60 million members of the French Community.

In 1961 the Department of Technical Cooperation was set up to coordinate British technical assistance to overseas countries, which was previously the job of the Foreign Office, the Commonwealth Relations Office, the Colonial Office, and the Ministry of Labour. The department, however, is not responsible for providing capital aid, and capital programmes continue to be administered by five separate Government departments. Because our programme of aid overseas has grown out of the Colonial Service its geographical distribution is distorted; and, although on a *per capita* basis we provide more aid than many other industrial countries this is still less than 1 per cent of our national income.

A large part of the British contribution to the underdeveloped countries has been private lending, which accounts for one third of the total. Britain has not been making nearly so much available in the form of Government soft loans – in 1961 France disbursed $953 million whereas the U.K. gave only $445 million by way of grants. This is important as it is the non-profitable investment in roads, schools, hospitals, and ports which will be required before private investment can be attracted to the less-developed regions. The Conservative Government has argued that 'soft loans' at below the going rates of interest distort competitive positions and weaken the function of interest rates in allocating resources among competing users. It is concerned that lending at 'soft' rates might have repercussions on the terms of Treasury lending to domestic borrowers such as the nationalized industries. Obviously a clear distinction should be made between 'soft' loan for infrastructure investment and money on which a return can be expected if it is properly used; apart from this a narrow Treasury view of the need to keep interest rates pure when applied to international aid is quite meaningless.

The ultimate aim should be a new aid partnership of the Western countries. If aid is channelled through a multi-lateral agency it is both more acceptable to the recipient countries and more effective as well, in so far as a coordinated programme of aid can be related to long-run development objectives of the developing countries. An international agency has also a better chance of insisting that aid is used in a more efficient manner. If one country tries to insist on the manner in which aid must be used it is liable to build up resentment and antagonism in the developing countries, but a quiet word from an international agency can work wonders, especially if there is no possibility that aid can be secured from another Western country as an alternative.

The developing countries also require skilled men and women to help carry out technical assistance programmes. The framework of the Colombo Plan should be extended to bring in other European countries and take in such regions as Africa, the Caribbean, and the Pacific, so that more aid can be made available to the underdeveloped countries on an equitable and coordinated basis. Britain could make a much greater contribution than we

are doing at present. Mr Grimond has called for a Commonwealth Service:

I might say that I personally regret that the West, and Her Majesty's
Government in particular, have not been able to build a fully professional service to fulfil these enormous demands for skilled personnel all over Africa, Asia, and, indeed, South America. We have only
to consider what happened in the Congo to see that the greatest and the
most urgent task of the Western world is to provide the skill to assist
these people to run their own countries. I am not talking about top-
level skills, but the teachers, the nurses, the managers, and all the
people who make up a civilized community. . . . There is a case for
bringing people from [Africa and Asia] into this country and for
sending people out to these territories. (*Hansard*, December 1962.)

The Government has rejected the idea of developing the
Colonial Service into an agency, covering the whole Commonwealth, available to any member country requiring technical or
administrative assistance. But something is certainly needed to
back up the efforts of the Department of Technical Cooperation,
giving it a pool of skilled manpower and experts to draw on.
The White Paper on recruitment for technical service overseas
issued in May 1962 had very little constructive to say. In Tan-
ganyika and Uganda former Colonial Office civil servants and
technical advisers are leaving at such a rate as to endanger the
administration and social services of the territories. It is a
tragedy that this country allowed its Colonial Service to run
down instead of trying to make it the foundations of an international service to supply administrators to these countries.

At present Britain does not train enough experts – particularly agriculturalists – with knowledge about the tropics, and
we do not give a good enough training to the students who
come here from the underdeveloped countries. According to the
Denning Report on Legal Education for Students from Africa
there were 824 from overseas in 1959. This represented an income to the Inns of Court of approximately £150,000, of which
some £42,000 is a deposit. Not only is this money unaccounted
for – the Inns of Court do not publish accounts – but the great
majority of students who pay the fees obtain little practical
benefit from their Inn except for library facilities. Apart from

the requirements that students eat dinner in Hall at least twelve times a year, and pay for it, the vast majority of overseas students might as well not exist after they have paid their fees for all the interest the Inns of Court take in them socially or educationally. Yet many of the future leaders of Africa and Asia study law at London. Much more needs to be done to devise special courses for Commonwealth students who come to Britain to study as well as provide more adequate hostel accommodation in order that they do not have to put up with racial prejudice during their leisure time. More could also be done to promote the exchange of personnel between member countries. Much more Government encouragement and assistance is needed in the educational, medical, and voluntary service fields. The British Council has reported that the overseas need for teachers is to be measured in thousands not hundreds, yet in 1961–2 only 226 were recruited. The Porritt Working Party on medical aid to the developing countries will be implemented by the Government 'so far as finance and demands on resources permit'; the Working Party stated that Great Britain is falling behind in its contribution to medical advance overseas.

All over Britain there are men and women with direct experience of the Commonwealth who could be persuaded to take part in an exchange of jobs if they did not lose their pension rights or their promotion prospects as a result. There is great scope especially for this kind of exchange in the education field but it will take a government with international aspirations to tap this kind of idealism. Too many people have been persuaded to think that the underdeveloped world is populated with Dagoes and Gyppoes.

A high level of capital aid and technical assistance with no ties attached is a necessary ingredient of closing the gap between the developed West and the underdeveloped world; but the primary need of these countries is markets. Aid, even on a massive scale, cannot close the widening gap. The average rate of growth of *per capita* income over the past decade in underdeveloped countries represents an annual rate of increase of less than $7 per head, while the average annual increase in the O.E.C.D. countries has been about $25 per head. The developing countries in the Commonwealth need markets – not just for their raw materials but for semi-manufactured and manufactured goods. One reason is that the fluctuations in the prices of commodities produced by the developing countries has cost them more over the past few years than all the funds they have obtained by way of aid. Britain must take the initiative in negotiating commodity agreements with the object of establishing the prices received by the developing Commonwealth countries for their raw materials. These agreements could only be negotiated in conjunction with the European Economic Community, which is a larger importer of Commonwealth raw material than Britain. Mr Wilson, who attacks the French Government as protectionist in one breath and calls for world commodity agreements in the next (as he did in a speech in Ottawa in February 1964), seems to overlook the fact that it was the French Government which mooted a world wheat agreement at the G.A.T.T. but it is the British Government which has shown the most reluctance to accept such an agreement.

The trouble with commodity agreements in the past is that they have been done on a commodity-by-commodity arrangement. An international development agency which was responsible for several commodity stabilization schemes would be able to use profits from the sales of one commodity to stabilize another which was under greater pressure. Furthermore only an agency which was able to forecast future trends and keep a sharp eye open for substitutes would be able to make a useful contribution. This is one area where the City of London with its network of commodity markets and merchant banks with special knowledge of overseas markets in the underdeveloped areas could make an important contribution. Up till now the City has always opposed any interference with the speculative character of the commodity markets on the grounds that support schemes would lead to prices being fixed permanently above 'equilibrium' levels. The absence of any strong pressure from the Government in favour of commodity stabilization has meant that the City pressure groups have so far swung the decisions. It is an interesting sidelight on the dual morality in politics today that whereas the rich countries accept that it is their duty to stabilize farm prices within a country, they do not find it such a good idea to stabilize commodity prices in the international markets which would benefit the people of the underdeveloped countries.

Even the stabilization of commodity prices would not be enough as too often the commodity itself is being replaced by a substitute. All the great traditional tropical products, cotton, jute, rubber, and tin, have had to face the fact that over the last twenty years the richer third of the world has discovered artificial substitutes or ways of managing with less. Secondly, if the underdeveloped countries are going to take off into a steady economic growth they must industrialize at least a sector of their economy in order that they can get the benefits of the increasing returns from manufactured industry and, at the same time, diversify their economy. Britain has a much better record than other countries in keeping a relatively open door for the manufactured goods of Asia and Africa, but by ourselves we can only satisfy a small percentage of the potential exports of the developing countries. Here again only international action can solve this important problem for the Commonwealth.

Regional common markets among the developing countries would permit greater specialization than would otherwise be possible. In Africa and Latin America the Western countries must encourage the people to set up regional partnerships of their own by giving aid to joint regional organizations, as with Marshall aid and the O.E.E.C. Liberals have called for a review, in conjuction with the other Commonwealth countries, of the present constitutional position of the remaining dependent territories, with the object of working out the best way to promote their political, economic, and social development. A number of these territories are too small and have too limited resources to be fully independent states on their own. Though no one solution can be appropriate in all cases, the proposed Federation of Malaysia illustrates what can be done when the countries concerned are able to work out their future together. Liberals have also pressed for the creation of some form of common service organization to take over certain federal functions of the Central African Federation. This could include postal and telegraph services, roads, and possibly health services.

The United Nations Economic Commission for Africa has put forward proposals for an African Common Market. As most of the African countries are too small to provide a market for new industries it follows that they must reach agreement among themselves if a wasteful duplication of investment is to be avoided. If this can be done – and the difficulties must not be underestimated – it could stimulate a much greater flow of trade between the African countries themselves, trade which at present tends to flow between Africa and the developed West. On the other hand a development of an African Common Market must involve discrimination against imports from the West in favour of African developing industries. Already the trade report of the U.N. Economic Commission for Africa shows that between 1961 and 1962 Africa's exports went up by 3 per cent while her imports went down by 3 per cent. The substitution of domestically manufactured goods for imported goods will be a continuing process in the developing countries which will have to be accepted in the West if the underdeveloped countries are to be allowed to develop. This is a frustrating experience for exporters who will no sooner develop a market for their exports than they will, by quota or by tariff, be replaced by local manufacturers. This will make for disintegrated trade between the two groups of countries unless there is a greater degree of international coordination of trade policies between regional blocks of nations as well as between individual countries. In the long run we must expect a spectacular increase in the imports of manufactured products originating in the poorer countries. As their only wealth is their plentiful low-wage manpower it will be necessary to envisage a large-scale redeployment of industrial activity which would entail a major reorientation of European industry.

Finally, more needs to be done to help the hungry. According to a paper read to the Royal Statistical Society by Dr Sukhature, the proportion of people suffering from under-nutrition in the world is between 10 and 15 per cent, or between 300 and 500 million people. Many more millions suffer from malnutrition – between one third and one half of the world's people, or nearly all the people in the underdeveloped regions. Meawnhile there are large agricultural surpluses piling up in the temperate countries of the developed world. Analyses of food needs and availabilities indicate that these conditions will probably continue for at least another decade. In most of the less-developed regions it seems unlikely that in the near future domestic agriculture will be able to expand as fast as the demand for food, which will rise rapidly owing to increases in both the population and the standard of living. The F.A.O. made a pilot study in India in 1955 of the use of food aid to promote development. It was found to be particularly useful where potential workers are unemployed or only partially employed between seed time and harvest. In this case the workers can be employed on development projects, and their increased demand for food may be offset by supplies under the aid programme. Their wages may then be paid partly in the form of food.

Again, the use of food aid to establish a food reserve in an underdeveloped country may also, besides its value as a safeguard against sudden food shortages, make a contribution to economic development. The possession of a large food reserve provides the planning authority with a certain elbow room, so that the failure of a domestic harvest does not immediately cause a food shortage and there is thus more time to take steps to deal with the situation. Another possibility suggested by the F.A.O. is that extra grain supplies could enable farmers to return land to grass and build up a base for sound livestock production. Feed grains could also be used directly to expand livestock production.

Since 1951 agricultural aid has accounted for a quarter of the total aid given under the Colombo Plan, mostly from the United States, which has provided more than £2,000 million of agricultural commodities; Canada and Australia have also provided agricultural commodities to the value of $64 million and $22 million respectively. Countries receiving this aid have undertaken to set aside the proceeds for use in economic development projects; for example the availability of Canadian wheat has helped to absorb the additional purchasing power resulting from the wages earned on development projects such as the Warsak hydro-electric and irrigation project in Pakistan, on which Canadian capital and technical assistance have also been concentrated. But the contribution could probably have been greater if food aid had been more fully integrated in the development plans of the receiving countries. It seems that the role of food aid so far has been that of mitigating shortages and enabling existing plans to be more fully developed rather than of raising the planned rate of development. A major reason for this is undoubtedly the fact that there has been until recently little assurance of the continuity of supplies, without which the developing countries are bound to hesitate before accelerating their development.

The Liberal Agricultural Committee called upon the British Government to take the initiative in securing a higher priority for food aid through the United Nations. In particular they drew attention to the desirability of using dried milk in programmes of food aid. So far aid has largely consisted of wheat and wheat flour. This has, in some cases, given rise to problems of adaptation in traditionally rice-eating countries, and while it has been an important contribution to relieving under-nutrition it has helped relatively little in dealing with the problem of malnutrition, which can be solved only through increased supplies of proteins.

Not only is there surplus capacity in the farming industry of the West, there is spare capacity in many industries. If surplus food can be produced in the West and given to the developing countries as a means of raising their living standards, it should not be beyond the wit of man to devise a system whereby credits can be given to the underdeveloped countries which they can use in any country in the Western world which finds itself with excess industrial capacity. It is not only in Britain where there are underemployed resources steaming from fear of unemployment. On the one hand each industrial country is scared to expand its domestic demand for fear of balance-of-payment difficulties, on the other hand there is the grinding poverty under which two thirds of mankind suffers. Under the present international economic arrangements the aid-giving institutions such as the International Development Association can only replenish their funds from grants from the wealthy nations of the West. To raise their contributions to the I.D.A. the developed nations must tax their citizens more; yet in most countries taxation is already high enough to be a brake on initiative and effort, so governments are reluctant to increase taxes to give more aid to underdeveloped countries. Moreover, those which are in deficit or even in bare balance – as Britain has been for some years – are afraid that to give any more will have an adverse effect on their balance of payments. They feel that they cannot afford to give any more, and the credit-worthiness of the under-developed countries is not such as to enable them to borrow more on economical terms; the result is deadlock.

The present situation in international economics is reminis-cent of the fear expressed by the Treasury men and the Central Bankers in the worst years of unemployment in the 1920s and 1930s: 'Of course we would like to help the unemployed but if we interfere with the system we shall only have a crisis of con-fidence and have more not less unemployment.' Nothing succeeds in times of crisis like the Conservative plea 'for God's sake don't change things – they will only get worse!'

Thanks to Keynes we now know that there is nothing inevi-table about the economic system. As long as we have our facts right there is every advantage in creating demand where there are unemployed resources. Why does the West not apply the same principles to the underdeveloped countries? Keynes himself proposed the establishment of an international bank at the end of the war which would have powers to create credit. The Americans would not agree. Now the world economy situa-tion has changed and it is the dollar which is under pressure and it is the United States which has the greatest potential which could be put to use by the developing countries. An initiative of this kind will not come from the United States, how-ever, where there is still a strong feeling that money which is not issued by a sovereign state or 'backed' in some mysterious way by gold or silver cannot be 'hard'.

The surplus European countries, especially Western Germany, are reluctant to agree to any scheme of international credit creation from the fear that it might add to their difficulties in controlling inflation. To create extra purchasing power on an international scale would be fine if the extra exports were called forth only from those countries which are in deficit and which have unused resources. But, it is argued, part of the extra pur-chasing power created as the result of giving credits to develop-ing countries will be spent in countries like Germany or France which are fully employed already, earn adequate surpluses, and which wish to decrease the rate at which they increase reserves.

But the real reason no country has seriously supported a scheme for creating international currency on a world scale is that a considerable surrender of sovereignty is involved. Imagine the reaction of the City of London if they thought that the British Government would try and get rid of sterling as an international reserve currency. This is what the creation of an international central bank able to create credit would mean. Unfortunately sterling has become identified in people's minds as a symbol of the Empire and Commonwealth. It is in fact a millstone round our necks. Look at the realities of sterling: it is a product of the depression. There was such a serious depression in the world that, when we devalued, other countries, hoping to keep their trade going at a slightly higher level than otherwise, went with us. Then the system was amplified because we incurred enormous war debts. Added to this, it is not an ideal reserve system for the sterling area at all. It has a bad exchange risk involved in it, far worse than if people held an international unit. Also it is a system that provides quite inadequate lending facilities. People are landed with a banker who never gives them an overdraft.

Britain has everything to gain from an increase in international liquidity. For too long a cautious obsession about the pound sterling has crippled our economic growth. Successive Conservative Chancellors have bowed down to the sacred totem of the City of London. The theory behind the stop-go policies was that monetary restraints and high bank rates reduce imports and stimulate exports so that the balance of payments is restored to surplus. But cutting down the home trade does not necessarily stimulate exports in the least. What it does is to reduce output, raise costs, and worsen our competitive position abroad. At the same time any reduction of imports creates a loss of purchasing power for our exports on the overseas markets. The Conservative reliance on classical monetary techniques has been fatuous and harmful and has raised the cost of servicing the national debt by some £200 million a year and our overseas sterling liabilities by £50 million.

It is quite likely that the Conservatives would still be advocating stop-go policies (as the only way of maintaining the value of the pound) if the nation – and particularly the New

Men – had not shown their complete opposition in a series of by-election reverses which culminated in Orpington.

The correct course is to take the initiative in launching an international plan for world development linked to an international credit scheme. Mr Maxwell Stamp, a former director of the International Monetary Fund, has shown how such a plan could operate. The Board of Governors of the I.M.F. would authorize the issue of Fund certificates to a value of $2 billion. The value of these certificates would be expressed in terms of gold but they would not be automatically convertible into gold.

Each member of the I.M.F. would agree to accept them when tendered by the Fund on a central bank and provide its own national currency in exchange. The holders of a Fund certificate would be able to exchange it at known rates into the currency of any country which is a member of the I.M.F. The I.M.F. would then give the certificates to an aid-coordinating agency which would allocate them to underdeveloped countries under an agreed programme. The countries receiving the certificates could use them to buy, say, machinery in Germany, the U.S., and the United Kingdom by tendering them to the central bank and acquiring Deutschmark, dollars, or sterling.

The management of international credit and currency on a world scale in this way would be a giant political step. It would make possible systematic joint policies for expansion and more effective transfer of resources to the underdeveloped world. But because it is a major political step it will depend on the solution of the healing of the divisions within the Alliance that exist today. The Anglo-Saxon countries, America and Britain, who have the two currencies that most need support, depend on continental Europe for a solution of the problem, for it is there that the other main source of exchange reserves is to be found. It thus remains a mockery for the Labour party to talk about the solutions to the world currency problem and at the same time snub the Common Market. This is one of the great fields where a pooling of sovereignty and an understanding of Europe is essential to the West.

The restoration of momentum to the movement for unity in the West is thus essential in defence, in economics, and to the gradual building up of a more stable society. The movement for unity in the West is indeed essential to world peace itself. For only when true political stability is achieved will Communism no longer be tempted to divide the West, and prove even readier than today to come to terms. Britain, though excluded from Europe, still occupies a key position in this Western strategy, and could give a new impetus to Western unity if it chose to do so. But both the Labour and Conservative parties have turned aside – the one to the myth of the independent deterrent, the other to virtually no policy at all. Liberalism, needed at home to restore purpose and drive to the nation, is needed even more to give this country a new creative role in the world at large.

Two other books published by Penguins
are described on the following pages

Voters, Parties, and Leaders
The Social Fabric of British Politics

Jean Blondel

Are we witnessing the end of class-barriers in the political behaviour of the British voter? Does the businessman vote like the railwayman, the white-collar worker like the unskilled labourer?

Of course they do not. But how different are their voting habits? Trade Unions are Labour-inclined, but all trade unionists are not Labour men. Are these non-Labour trade unionists exceptional? And, at the other end of the scale, are labour-inclined professional people, managers, and executives rare but interesting exceptions?

These are some of the questions which the newly appointed Professor of Government in the University of Essex attempts to answer in this original book. In examining the background, outlook, and interests of voters, party members, politicians, civil servants, and party leaders, and endeavouring to trace some of the subtle threads that tie certain individuals to certain organizations, he presents an anatomy of the political world. And he asks: 'What is the "Establishment" we talk of? Does it exist? And if so, does it rule?'

What's Wrong with Parliament?

Andrew Hill and Anthony Whichelow

Is Parliament receiving the right information to enable it to decide and control in the conditions of today?

The principal purpose of the House of Commons is – as it always was – to control public spending. Amid the complex legislation and astronomical budgets of a modern state, however, a busy debating-society of some 600 overworked members can be little more than a rubber-stamp, adding the initials of democracy at the foot of the government's bill. How, we may ask, can the unqualified representatives of the people presume to decide issues which may, at root, call for expert scientific understanding?

The two authors of this Penguin Special have made a close study of Parliament's workings. They believe this historic institution can be made to fulfil its intended function today, and they show how, with a fuller service of information, the Commons could be briefed to scrutinize more effectively the action of the Executive. Their suggestions for improving that effectiveness are reasonable, practicable, and well-informed.